THE
NORMANDY
CAMPAIGN

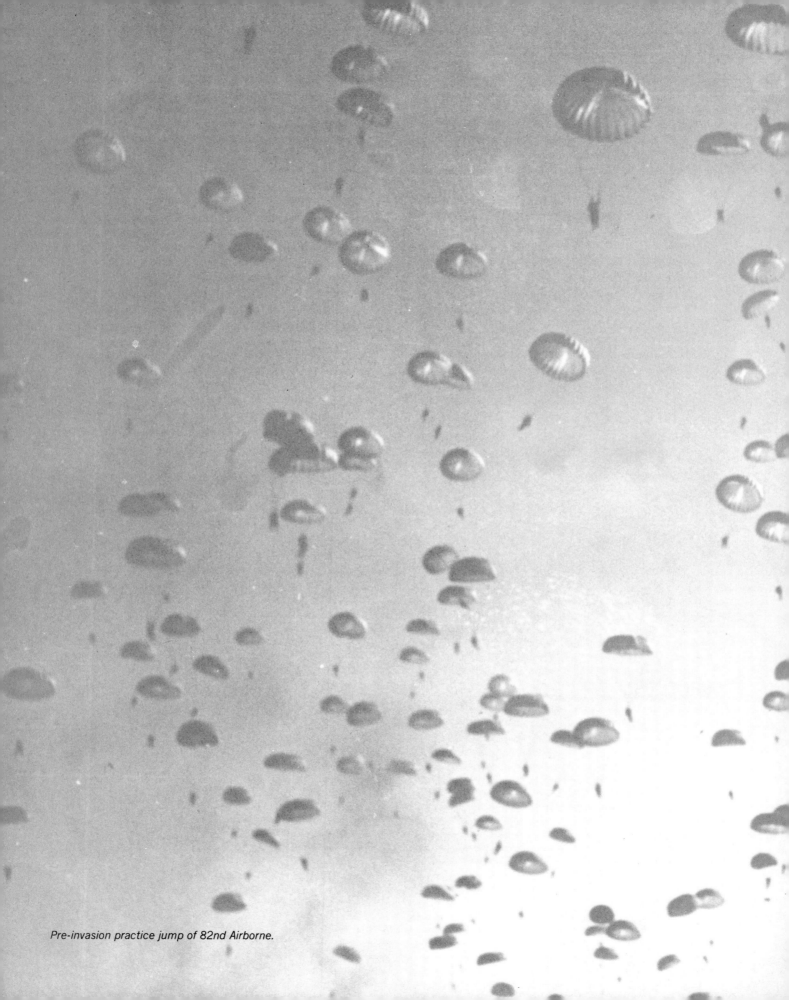

Pre-invasion practice jump of 82nd Airborne.

THE
NORMANDY CAMPAIGN

June and July, 1944

Stephen A. Patrick

GALLERY BOOKS
An imprint of W.H. Smith Publishers Inc.
112 Madison Avenue
New York, New York 10016

Prepared by Combined Books, P.O. Box 577,
Conshohocken, PA 19428

Project Coordinator: Robert Pigeon

Editor of the Series: Albert A. Nofi

Photographs by U.S. Army, Signal Corps, and courtesy
of U.S. Army Military History Institute and National
Archives.

We gratefully acknowledge the help and support of the
following talented individuals: Antoinette Bauer,
Kenneth S. Gallagher, Gary and Mary Sue Gross and
Edward Wimble.

Maps by Kevin Wilkins

Design by Lizbeth Hoefer-Nauta and Kirsten Kerr.

Produced by Wieser & Wieser, Inc.
118 East 25th Street, New York, NY 10010.

This edition published by Gallery Books, an imprint of
W.H. Smith Publishers, Inc., 112 Madison Avenue,
New York, NY 10016.

Library of Congress Cataloging-in-Publication Data

Patrick, Stephen A.
    The Normandy campaign, June and July, 1944.

    (The Great military campaigns of history)
    1. World War, 1939-1945 — Campaigns — France —
Normandy.
2. Normandy (France) — History. I. Title. II. Series.
D756.5.N6P35 1986   940.54'21   86-6547

ISBN 0-8317-6420-1

Senior U.S. officers tour beaches June 14th.

CONTENTS

From the Dustbin of History

Ste. Mère-Eglise from the southwest. Its command of surrounding terrain is obvious.

Maps

U.S. soldier gazes toward his objective beneath the cliffs of Normandy.

★The Great Military Campaigns of History★

PREFACE TO THE SERIES

Jonathan Swift termed war "that mad game the world so loves to play". He had a point. Universally condemned, it has nevertheless been almost as universally practiced. For good or ill, war has played a significant role in the shaping of history. Indeed, there is hardly a human institution which has not in some fashion been influenced and molded by war, even as it helped shape and mold war in turn. Yet the study of war has been as remarkably neglected as its practice has been commonplace. With a few outstanding exceptions, the history of wars and of military operations has until quite recently been largely the province of the inspired patriot or the regimental polemicist. Only in our times have serious, detailed, and objective accounts come to be considered the norm in the treatment of military history and related matters. Yet there still remains a gap in the literature, for there are two types of military history. One type is written from a very serious, highly technical, professional perspective and presupposes that the reader is deeply familiar with background, technology, and general situation. The other is perhaps less dry, but merely lightly reviews the events with the intention of informing and entertaining the layman. The qualitative gap between the two is vast. Moreover, there are professionals in both the military and in academia whose credentials are limited to particular moments in the long, sad history of war, and there are laymen who have a more than passing understanding of the field; and then there is the concerned citizen, interested in understanding the phenomenon in an age of unusual violence and unprecedented armaments. It is to bridge the gap between the two types of military history, and to reach the professional and the serious amateur and the concerned citizen alike, that this series, *The Great Campaigns of Military History*, is designed.

The individual volumes of *The Great Campaigns of Military History* are each devoted to an intensive examination of a particularly significant military operation. The focus is not on individual battles, but on campaigns, on the relationship between movements and battles and how they fit within the overall framework of the war in question. By making use of a series of innovative techniques for the presentation of information, *The Great Campaigns of Military History* can satisfy the exacting demands of the professional and the serious amateur, while making it possible for the concerned citizen to understand the events and the conditions under which they developed. This is accomplished in a number of ways. Each volume contains a substantial, straight-forward narrative account of the campaign under study. This is supported by an extensive series of modular "sidebars". Some are devoted to particular specific technical matters, such as weaponry, logistics, organization, or tactics. These modules each contain detailed analyses of their topic, and make considerable use of "hard" data, with many charts and tables. Other modules deal with less technical matters, such as strategic analysis, anecdotes, personalities, uniforms, and politics. Each volume contains several detailed maps, supplemented by a number of clear, accurate sketchmaps, which assist the reader in understanding the course of events under consideration, and there is an extensive set of illustrations which have been selected to assist the reader still further. Finally, each volume contains materials designed to help the reader who is interested in learning more. But this "bibliography" includes not merely a short list of books and articles related to the campaign in question. It also contains information on study groups devoted to the subject, on films which deal with it, on recordings of period music, on simulation games and skirmish clubs which attempt to recreate the tactics, on museums where one can have a first-hand look at equipment, and on tours of the battlefields. The particular contents of each volume will, of course, be determined by the topic in question, but each will provide an unusually rich and varied treatment of the subject. Each volume in *The Great Campaigns of Military History* is thus not merely an account of a particular military operation, but it is a unique reference to the theory and practice of war in the period in question.

The Great Campaigns of Military History is a unique contribution to the study of war and of military history, which will remain of interest and use for many years.

Ike goes ashore, June 7th.

CHAPTER I

THE PRELIMINARIES

To defeat Nazi Germany, the Western Allies had to mount the largest amphibious attack in history. Nothing like it in size had ever been attempted. Failure would mean prolonging the war, at best. At worst it would give the enemy a chance to develop the "wonder weapons" they had been talking about which might turn the tide in favor of Germany and cost the Allies the war.

The Allied Plan

Although invasion of Europe became a goal for the western Allies from the time Hitler declared war on the United States, December 12, 1941, it was not until May of 1943, at the Trident Conference between the United States and Britain, in Washington, that a formal date of May 1, 1944, was fixed. There had been serious discussion of invasion in 1943 but, largely because the U.S. thought it was too soon, 1944 became the earliest practical time. In fact, in March 1942, Dwight D. Eisenhower as head of the American War Plans Division, had presented the Chief of Staff, George C. Marshall, with two plans for the invasion of Europe. One, codenamed Sledghammer, proposed an emergency landing of five divisions in the fall of 1942, in the event that Russia showed signs of collapsing. The other, called Roundup, was for a major invasion on April 1, 1943, between Boulogne and Le Havre, for thirty American and eighteen British divisions. These 1.5 million men would require some 7,000 landing craft, which were then still unbuilt and well down the Navy's priority list. Given the apparent dire straits of Russia in the fall of 1942, with Leningrad still under seige and the Germans slowly taking Stalingrad, it is hard to imagine what other indicators of Soviet collapse were needed if Sledgehammer was seriously considered. Apparently, it was not. Roundup also disappeared, if only because the kind of forces required could not possibly be mustered in 1943. It should not be forgotten, however, that the ultimate plan chose essentially the same landing area.

An invasion of a defended coastline had never before been successful. The German occupied side of the English Channel had been fortified, after a fashion, not long after the defeat of France and once it became apparent that an invasion of France across the English Channel was being planned, these fortifications were strengthened. The British had their own bitter experience landing against a fortified position in Gallipoli, in 1915. They had been pinned down and, after an extended period of heavy losses, were forced to pull out. In 1942 a landing had been made at Dieppe. That had been even less successful. Many believed it was simply impossible to mount an amphibious operation against a defended coastline. But, if the Allies were to get back into France, they had no choice.

Planning for the invasion actually began before a date was fixed. British Lt. Gen. Fredrick E. Morgan was designated Chief of Staff to the Supreme Allied Commander (designate) or COSSAC, as the title was abbreviated. He assembled the people who made the plan for the invasion and as a result, the term COSSAC tended to be extended to include the whole group involved in the planning. Morgan had been selected, in part, because he got along well with the Americans. Experiences in inter-allied operations in World War I had not gone too well and both the U.S. and Britain knew they had to work well together if they were going to beat Germany. By June 1943, COSSAC had made its most important decision: it selected Normandy

German gun emplacement under construction prior to D-Day.

as the site of the landings. From that the rest of the planning could follow.

While the officers who led the actual fighting have, justly, received the fame, it cannot be overstated that without the work of COSSAC, it would never have happened. Through hard work and, in many cases, intelligent guessing, they managed to piece together a plan which accomplished the impossible—a successful landing on a defended coast and, in the process, made victory possible.

Even as the planning was going on, steps were taken to flesh out the forces available. The British activated 21st Army Group in mid-1943 and gave it control of not only the home defenses but the British side of the invasion. In November it became directly involved in the planning of the landings, handling the land side of the operation. It had been decided between Churchill and Eisenhower that because the Americans would be putting in the larger share of troops, the over-all command would go to an American. However, because the British had

more combat experience against the Germans, the initial ground command would go to a British officer. On December 6, 1943, President Roosevelt selected Dwight D. Eisenhower to fill the position of Supreme Commander, Allied Forces. The obvious choice should have been Marshall, who certainly wanted the command, but Roosevelt thought him too valuable to allow out of Washington. All things considered, he may have been right. Eisenhower proved successful in his assigned role and it is questionable whether Marshall's successor would have handled that end of the operation as well. Eisenhower had been in charge of the landings in North Africa as well as in Sicily and had shown his ability to get along with the British, including their testy hero, Bernard L. Montgomery. As it turned out, shortly thereafter, Montgomery was given command of 21st Army Group which meant, in effect, that he would be the British officer who commanded all the ground forces, both American and British, in the initial phases. Montgomery's selection

Montgomery and Major General Gale south of Breville two days before the opening of Operation Goodwood.

was somewhat of a surprise in military circles because he was not regarded as the British general best suited for the role. Alexander was considered more able by both Prime Minister Winston Churchill and Eisenhower. However, Alexander was involved in Italy. The Chief of the Imperial General Staff, Alan Brooke, pushed for Montgomery, on the strength of his performance in North Africa. Moreover, regardless of military prestige, Montgomery's public prestige was so high that he was the natural selection.

It was not until December, 1943, that COS-

SAC was given a better fix on the forces available. What they had been working on was the assumption that only three divisions would be used to secure the initial beachhead. The COS-SAC plan was to land the United States First Army in the area between the Orne and Vire rivers, what later became Gold and Juno beaches. Elements from three different corps were to be involved—one American, one British and one Canadian. As the bridgehead built up, somewhere around D+7, the Canadian First Army would be inserted on the eastern side and

U.S. soldiers train with flame-throwers against pillboxes in England. October, 1943. Many units lost more men in training accidents than they did on D-Day.

the U.S. First Army would assume control over American troops only. The Americans would then swing west and north to take Cherbourg by D+25, then back south, eventually clearing Britanny. The British and the Canadians were expected to break out to the east, securing a line roughly from Rouen to Paris, as well as the key port of Le Havre. For the landing, two British parachute brigades were to be dropped near Caen to cover the east flank of the landings and seven U.S. parachute battalions were to go in to attack coastal batteries and secure passages in-

land, ahead of the invasion. To support this air landing, COSSAC felt that 799 troop-carrying aircraft would be required.

In September, 1943, Brig. Gen. James Gavin, who had led the 82d Airborne Division in Sicily, joined COSSAC and strongly criticized the idea of landing separate battalions. He had personal experience in the difficulty of linking up on the ground and began to push for a revision which would concentrate the airbore landings in a more compact area.

In December, 1943, both Eisenhower and

Just like the real thing. British pioneered realistic training with line ammunition in pre-invasion exercises such as this one.

Montgomery agreed that the three-division landing provided too narrow a front. Montgomery wanted to expand the planned landing front from 25 miles to 50 miles. He also felt it important to have at least two corps headquarters involved for both Britain and the U.S., with two more divisions, making a total of five in the initial landing. Further, these were to be supplemented by airborne landings inland, to screen the flanks of the seaborne landings.

Expanding the number of divisions threw a lot of COSSAC's calculations out since all of the logistical support would have to be refigured. The major problem would be getting enough shipping to land all of the people and equipment in that first wave. It was the British who originally conceived the idea of the various landing craft used at Normandy, though the scope of the building project was one which only the American shipyards could handle. Initially, even they couldn't handle it because they were tied up building cargo ships and ships for anti-submarine warfare. However, once it became obvious that without the landing craft, the invasion couldn't occur, space was shifted to build the various ships and boats required. Nonetheless, because something on the order of 270 of these vessels were required, it ultimately pushed the target date back from May 1, 1944 to June 1, 1944. In all, Montgomery's revisions pushed the whole naval requirement from roughly 3,000 ships to 4,000. At the same time, the requirements for air transport were increased to 880 aircraft. However, unlike shipping, aircraft production in the U.S. was booming and it was estimated that some 1,022 C-47's would be available, as well as 218 converted RAF bombers and 3,300 gliders of all types, both U.S. and British.

As was the practice, a code name was assigned the actual invasion. It was called Overlord. The specific plans for the landings fell under the code name Neptune. COSSAC handled the Overlord planning but Neptune was passed on to the organizations more directly involved, such as Montgomery's 21st Army Group. The planning for the landings was projected for the first fifteen days by the Neptune planners. The difficulty in such planning is obvious. In attempting to do what had never been done before, they could not draw directly on other operations. Yet, the accuracy of their planning had to be fairly close if they were to avoid disaster. If they overestimated the speed with which they would advance on land, troops and supplies from the follow-up waves would pile up and create a catastrophic traffic jam. If they underestimated either the speed of advance or the rate of expenditure of supplies, including ammunition, they could find themselves overextended or out of ammunition or unable to take advantage of a key weakness, any one of which might allow the Germans to recover and bottle them up on the beaches. Both sides saw the key to the battle as being able to get off the beaches and inland in good order. If they were unable to do that, the Allies would be pushed back into the sea. If they were successful, they had the open countryside of France and could use their greater numbers to break open the Germans. So the planning was critical in a way that few military plans need to be.

Fixing the exact date of the landing was actually an easy task, simply because a series of quite unrelated factors combined to leave few alternatives. The planners did not want to land

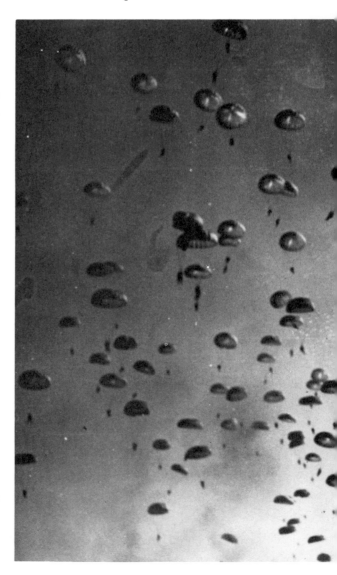

at high tide or with a falling tide because they wanted the rising tide to float the beached landing craft off so that they could go back for another wave of troops. On the other hand, they didn't want to land too near dead low water because that meant about 300 meters of additional beach which would have to be crossed under enemy fire. The problem was further compounded when the Germans began to place obstacles, first above the high water mark and then below the high water mark. The Allies had to time their landing so that the tide would let the first wave out short of the obstacles—not so far away that they could be cut up before reaching them and no so close that the would be landed right in the teeth of the obstacles. Moreover, since the obstacles were designed to hinder landings, they had to make sure the tide was not yet in so far that the landing craft would be damaged by the obstacles. Montgomery fi-

nally decided that the landing should occur about three hours before high tide. These obstacles so concerned the Neptune planners that they were persuaded to develope a special kind of tank, known as a Duplex Drive (DD) tank. This would have a special flotation device which would have a propeller, powered by the tank's engine. On landing, that gear would be shed and the tank would move as normal. For some reason, they did not give much consideration to using the amphibious tanks developed by the U.S. for Pacific operations.

One element they did draw upon from the Pacific was a recognition that there would have to be a major bombardment of the shore, both by naval and aerial elements, with the goal of pinning down any defenders who could fire on the landings and interdicting possible reinforcements which were inland and might try to get to the beaches. For the navy, this meant they had

Pre-invasion practice jump of 82nd Airborne.

to have daylight. At the same time, the navy wanted to have the cover of darkness to cross the channel. These factors narrowed the possible landing days to those when there would be a rising tide at around sun-up. The airborne landings added another factor. They would go in in darkness, before the amphibious landings hit the beaches. They wanted a full moon for those landings so that the paratroopers, once on the ground, could link up and be in position to assist the landings. Without a moon, link-up before daylight would be virtually impossible. The first available days, after the target date of June 1, were June 5 through 7, 1944. The next such combination was another month off.

In addition to the D.D. tanks, the Overlord planners considered a more critical problem. Although they hoped to take Cherbourg by D+15, in the meantime they needed a means to off-load supplies. They came up with the notion of "portable" harbors. Known as "Mulberry", the harbor would consist of a series of floatable piers which would be towed over to the beachhead and sunk in place, allowing the deep water cargo ships to stand off the beach and yet land their supplies of vehicles, ammunition and the like.

When the five divisional beaches were marked out, it was apparent that those on the east, around Caen, had a fair amount of open country in front of them. On the other hand, the two western beaches were facing an area which had not only been flooded by the Germans, but was also criss-crossed by heavy hedgerows, known as bocage. Ideally, given the greater mobility their forces had, the Americans should have gone on the left or eastern side of the landings, but for several reasons, it was ultimately decided the British would have the left and the Americans the right. As they advanced eastward after they broke out, this would make for more effective lines of communications. The British would be closest to Britain, whereas the Americans, who would be drawing their supplies from the U.S., would not need to be as concerned about that. A serious problem was that the British Army didn't have much in the way of reserves. A bloody battle to get out of the bocage was simply easier for the Americans to absorb than the British. As a result, the British got the three eastern-most beaches, which they named Sword, Juno, and Gold with the Canadians actually having responsibility for Juno. The Americans got the western two beaches, initially named X and Y, then Omaha and Oregon, and finally Omaha and Utah. Utah was seen as the

Mulberry: They Said It Couldn't Be Done

One of the most interesting developments for the invasion was the artificial harbors, generally known by the over-all cover name of "Mulberry." Actually, Mulberry was made up of several components. First, there was "Gooseberry." Gooseberry was the name applied to a number of worn-out merchantmen which were to be sunk in a line starting as far in shore as they could go and then running out to sea in an arc to provide a breakwater.

Extending seaward from the Gooseberry ships was a series of floating concrete caissons, known as "Phoenix." These would be sunk outside the Gooseberry ships with their upper surfaces projecting above the water. A series of cruciform steel floats, given the code name "Bombardon" were moored outside the harbor formed by the Gooseberries and Phoenixes, to act as a floating breakwater. Running from the Gooseberries onto the actual beaches were a series of metal piers which would rise and fall with the tide and were known as "Whales."

The net result was an "instant" harbor, approximately 2.5 km wide, over which the Allies could unload the merchant ships to supply the beaches. Mulberry-A was set for Omaha, located opposite Colleville, and Mulberry-B for Gold, at Arromanches.

In all, the Mulberries took ten days to assemble. Although Mulberry-A was effectively destroyed by the storm two days after it was complete, Mulberry-B, although damaged by the storm, proved highly useful in landing supplies. Indeed, until Cherbourg was secured and made operational, it was the only effective means of landing supplies to the Allied troops.

Above: *U.S. gliders prior to being attached to towing aircraft. Chalked unit numbers on sides are to aid assembly on landing zones.*

more critical of the U.S. beaches. It was on the Cotentin Peninsula and the forces landing there had the mission of taking the port of Cherbourg by D + 15. It was anticipated that Cherbourg would be the major port for supply until a larger port, such as Antwerp or Brest could be captured.

The British were to land three infantry divisions on their beaches, reinforced by an armored brigade at each beach, as well as the DD tanks out of the 79th Armoured Division, a specially formed division which carried the DD tanks as well as other experimental armor. The British beaches lay between the mouth of the Orne River, on the east, and Arromanches on the west. To assist the landing, the British 6th Airborne Division was to land east of the Orne. The overall command of the British elements was given to Lt. Gen. Sir Miles Dempsey and his Second Army.

The Americans would be under First Army, commanded by Lt. Gen. Omar N. Bradley. At Omaha Beach he planned to land V Corps under Maj. Gen. Leonard T. Gerow, with 1st

Left: *Even crude obstacles could be formidable, especially at high tide.*

Aerial view gives some idea of construction and layout of Mulberry artificial harbor.

Infantry Division as its spearhead, augmented by a regimental combat team from 29th Inf. Div. The remainder of the 29th would land in the second wave. At Utah, VII Corps, under J. Lawton Collins, would send in 4th Inf. Div. Because it was important to get to Cherbourg, the U.S. airborne operations were put in support of Utah. 101st Airborne Div. was to secure the routes off the beach while 82d Abn. Div. was to land at the base of the Cotentin Peninsula and seal it off.

To provide adequate support, the planners requested twelve battleships or cruisers and another hundred destroyers. This was, in fact, more than both the Royal Navy and the U.S. Navy could provide. Initial control of this fleet would be under the British Admiral Ramsey.

However, he calculated that he would have to divert a portion of his force to screen against German attempts to disrupt the landings out of the North Sea. That further depleted the ships available. Finally, the U.S. Navy was prevailed upon to send over three pre-World War I battleships—*Arkansas*, *Texas*, and *Nevada*, this last a survivor of Pearl Harbor. Ultimately they had two bombardment fleets, the first consisting of *Nevada*, a British monitor, two American and one British heavy cruisers, two British light cruisers, eight American destroyers and a Dutch gunboat, while the other consisted of *Arkansas*, *Texas*, two British and two French light cruisers, and nine American and three British destroyers. At that they calculated a need for more than 7,000 tons of explosives, of which the naval force

could only provide somewhat over 2,000. The rest would come out of the air elements in support of the landings.

Even as the day grew near, last minute revisions were required. Aerial reconnaissance showed German Field Marshal Erwin Rommel's defensive efforts to deter invasion. They found, in April, obstacles on all of the major landing sites proposed for the 82d Airborne. So, while they had originally planned a lift of 410 gliders to go in with the division in its initial landing and 260 for the 10st Airborne, this was revised to 50 gliders for each division on the initial landings, another 200 on the evening of D-Day, another 100 for 82d Airborne on the morning of D+1 and yet another on the evening of D+1. The mission of the 82d was changed as well.

Pilings for beach obstacles pounded deep to anchor on firmer ground. The tide has caught up with a late afternoon work party.

Wooden defenses such as these were little hindrance to the armored assault vehicles of the British 79th Armored Division. The Americans paid less attention to specialized vehicles, to their cost on D-Day.

Originally scheduled to land near St. Sauveur-le-Vicomte, on the west of the Cotentin Peninsula, they were instead to secure crossings over the Merderet River, capture the road center at Ste. Mere-Eglise and assist VII Corps in rapidly moving in from the beaches, as Montgomery now expected them to take Cherbourg by D+9 and their official time table was cut in half from D+29 to D+14.

Aerial view of beaches, showing shell craters from pre-invasion bombardment.

German beach obstacles under construction. Two men at left wear white fatigue trousers.

Fortitude: Patton

In examining potential Allied landing areas, it really took little imagination for the Germans to limit probable choices to just two: the Pas de Calais and Normandy. There were some obvious considerations for any amphibious landing. It should be within range of fighter cover. It should have sufficient capacity to unload the necessary troops to accomplish the landing. The sea crossings should be as short as possible. A final consideration was the amount of German resistance to be expected. Both the Pas de Calais and Normandy fulfilled all of these requirements. Indeed, the Pas de Calais was the single best target area insofar as air cover, suitable landing sites and length of sea crossing. But because it was so obviously the best choice, the element of surprise would be virtually impossible to attain. At least in the initial going, the Germans would have the edge in that they could bring forces against the beachhead, while the landing troops were still so restricted they lacked room to maneuver. The Calais position allowed not only the *Fifteenth Army* to send its troops in, but also allowed *Seventh Army* to shift eastward.

An appraisal of the Normandy area noted that the area around Caen would be good tank country but the area westward of Caen, toward the Cotentin peninsula, had marshy river valleys near the coast and steep hills and narrow valleys in the highlands, all of which made it unsuitable for tanks. From the Allied point of view, this was an advantage. Being penned in on a narrow beach in the early going, the Allies would not have the room to maneuver armor in any event. Their major tank interest, then, was in restricting enemy use of its tanks. Normandy did this. Although it didn't meet some of the criteria as well as the Pas de Calais, it met them well enough to work.

Again, though, it required little imagination for the Germans to reach the same conclusion and concentrate forces around both the Pas de Calais and Normandy. It is not surprising then that the

"Rattle" conference, held in Scotland on June 28, 1943, selected Normandy as the landing site and also immediately set plans in operation to deceive the Germans as to their true intentions.

The deception plan was one of many the Allies developed during the war. Ironically, most of them didn't work that well. They had done some elaborate work in 1943 without the Germans showing one sign of reaction to it. Now they had a most difficult task. It is one thing to devise a deception plan which will make the enemy think you are attacking at a logical place while you then attack by surprise from an unexpected area. It is quite another to try to convince the enemy that you were going to make your attack in every place but the logical one.

This deception plan was known as "Fortitude" and was actually subdivided into Fortitude North and Fortitude South. Fortitude was to carry on past the landings until around July 20 as it was also important, assuming the landings got ashore in good order, to keep the Germans thinking that there might be other landings and that this was just part of a multiple thrust operation. More precisely, they wanted to convince the Germans that the main landing could not be made until late July, at the earliest.

One concern was that the Germans had some 27 divisions located in Norway and Denmark, simply doing nothing. The Allies wanted to ensure they stayed there and so they devised Fortitude North. The purpose of Fortitude North was to suggest to the Germans a major landing in Norway, to take place either before or after a landing in France. The unit assigned to this would be the British Fourth Army, located in Scotland. In fact, the largest unit ever assigned to the British Fourth Army was a battalion given the mission of simulating traffic. To augment Fourth Army was U.S. XV Corps. The XV Corps was a real corps but assigned elsewhere, as well as a British II Corps at Stirling and VII Corps at Dundee.

The real centerpiece of Fortitude was Fortitude South. Probably the most elaborate effort went into Fortitude South of any deception operation in history. As with Fortitude North, most of the units in Fortitude South were non-existant. But they took on all of the flavor of real units.

Fortitude South was built around the "First U.S. Army Group" (FUSAG). FUSAG was commanded by Lt. Gen. George S. Patton, Jr. Patton, of course, was well known for his activity in North Africa and Sicily and he was very well regarded by the Germans as an extremely difficult enemy. To tie the two Fortitudes together, British Fourth Army would join FUSAG after the landings in Norway. FUSAG was located in a triangle formed by Dover-Canterbury-King's Lynne, eastern Kent.

Considerable effort was undertaken to create a simulated army. Overnight tank parks developed, thanks to carefully painted balloons. They might not look like much up close but from the height the Germans had to fly for their aerial recon, they passed muster easily. To add to the flavor, real tanks were regularly run around to create tank tracks on the ground. To support the "army" a fleet of ships, of course, had to exist. For this they called out the British motion picture industry and had them create a spectacular simulation of ships out of tubing, painted canvas, and steel drums. These were stuffed into every plausible body of water, just as if they were really massing to ship FUSAG at some other date. The "crews" of these ships had to be visible so they took soldiers who were unfit for combat and had them play the role.

The target of FUSAG was the Pas de Calais. This being the more suitable of the two most likely areas, the hope was that the Germans would swallow FUSAG and not tip any reports they might get about a landing in Normandy.

There were plans afoot to lay a pipeline across the English channel in order to supply fuel. Accordingly,

Leads a Paper Army

FUSAG had to have its pipeline. A tremendous pier was built at Dover to act as the British end of this pipeline. It was, again, made out of canvas and wood. However, to make sure it looked realistic, one of Britain's foremost archetects was called in to design it. The work was ostentatiously inspected by the King, by Eisenhower and Montgomery, with public acclaim given to the men working on it. This did not go unnoticed by the Germans. As Dover lay within the range of their large artillery, the Germans would periodically shell it. To make the Germans feel good about their efforts, rounds which came close produced sodium fires which burned with all the intensity to be expected of a real target.

By this time, the Allies had gained command of the air over Britain. But it would hardly do any good to go through this elaborate deception plan if no one saw it. Accordingly, German reconnaissance efforts were allowed to penetrate into the FUSAG area, though kept at an appropriate altitude to be sure they couldn't get enough detail in their photographs to show it was all a sham.

Perhaps the cleverest piece dealt with radio traffic. The Allies knew the Germans had radios capable of monitoring military radio traffic in Britain. Their goal was to keep radio traffic non-existant in the 21st Army Group, which would really lead the invasion, but make it appear quite normal in FUSAG. To assist in this, they ran wires from Montgomery's headquarters in Portsmouth, to Dover the nominal headquarters for FUSAG and put the transmissions out through antennas in Dover. As a result, Montgomery's headquarters could send normal traffic to subordinate elements but as far as the German radio direction finders were concerned, all of this was coming from the FUSAG area. The whole operation was given a patina of reality by having letters printed in the paper from irate Englishmen complaining about the foreigners overrunning the countryside.

Although the indications are that Fortitude North never really impressed the Germans, Fortitude South did. Part of this has to go to the credit of the British XX Committee, or "Double Cross" committee, an organization under British Intelligence, which managed to run the German spy network in Britain. Through diligence, they had put out of operation some of the German spies but their real-coup was to make many of these spies into double agents. As a result, they, too, were forwarding reports about FUSAG. Getting these reports from "reliable informants" along with the aerial photographs make it very hard not to believe in FUSAG.

One of the great difficulties in intelligence work is clearing the mind of preconceived notions and simply looking at the picture being presented. No one, apparently, was disturbed by the fact that their recon planes could get looks at Kent relatively easily but were met with stiff resistance when they tried to get over the area where the true build-up was occuring. Nor did they seem concerned about the apparent lack of security exhibited by FUSAG. Why were they making no effort to keep radio silence? Why were the British printing the letters from angry citizens about the foreigners. Maybe they just dismissed some of these things as foolish Anglo-Saxon sentimentality, keeping alive civil liberties in the direst of straits. The point is that Fortitude South fit in well with the pre-conceived notion of the German high command. They thought that the Pas de Calais was the proper place to make a landing and could see no reason why the Allies should not, also. Here, then, was proof positive that they and the Allies were thinking along the same lines. All they discovered fit their pattern and therefore they could throw out things which didn't seem to fit. In the eternal chicken-egg game intelligence people play, the Germans never seem to have answered satisfactorily why, if the Pas de Calais was so obviously the best choice, the Allies should not realize the Germans would think so too and defend

accordingly. But that reasoning can go on in a circle forever—maybe the Allies thought the Pas de Calais was so obvious that the Germans wouldn't believe they would try there—and so they would land there.

Whatever the reason, Fortitude South worked. The Germans shifted no troops of note into the Normandy area. Certainly the few units located there could not be anything more than a mild precaution, just in case they were wrong, rather than a heart-felt belief that it was Normandy and not the Pas de Calais.

Once the landings went in, the last piece of Fortitude was in convincing the Germans that Normandy was not THE landing and that an even bigger one was due under FUSAG. As a result, FUSAG was protrayed as even larger than 21st Army Group. Thus, if the Germans deduced the size and organization of 21st Army Group, they might still hold their units in place in anticipation of FUSAG's landing.

In fact, it appears that Fortitude South was an unqualified success because the Germans did react slowly and were very reluctant to release the strategic reserves, something which only can be explained by a fear that the major landings were yet to come. Because of Fortitude, the Allies were able to deceive the Germans and achieve that critical element of surprise which made success possible.

The German Side

France, in 1944, was considered a quiet zone by the Germans. Two basic categories of troops were there: the permanent garrison troops and troops back for rest and refitting. The garrison troops were divisions which had been stationed there, some since the end of the operations against France in 1940, and had nominally been placed to screen against Allied attempts to invade the continent, as well as constituting the army of occupation. They had been on alert for four years and the sense of urgency was weak—a classic example of crying "wolf" too many times. The rest and refit units were elements which had been mauled on the eastern front and were sent to France to be brought back up to strength. The thought of being kept in the west to counter an invasion was far from their minds.

German intelligence knew something was afoot. They knew that Britain and the U.S. had pulled some strong divisions out of the Mediterranean and sent them to Britain, notably the British 1st and 7th Armoured, 1st Airborne, and 51st Highland Divisions, as well as the American 1st and 9th Infantry Divisions. Also, they detected the movement of a large number of landing craft and other vessels from the Mediterranean to Britain.

Generalfieldmarshall (Gmf) Erwin Rommel, recuperated from the illness which had caused him to be absent from the final fighting in North Africa, was in charge of *Heeresgruppe (Army Group) B,* under the control of *Oberbefehlshaber West (OB West),* commanded by the venerable Gfm Gerd von Rundstedt. Rommel's command included Holland, Belgium, and France down to the Loire, on the west coast. The remainder of France was under the control of

Processing prisoners, June 8. Most German tunics worn late in the war had unpleated pockets for ease of manufacture.

8th Infantry Division troops wade through area flooded by Germans to slow Allied advance.

HG G, commanded by Generaloberst Blaskowitz. As might be expected of a general who had made his reputation by the offensive, Rommel was urging that steps be taken to harass the buildup by sending U-boats against the shipping in the harbors, mining the harbors, and bombing the troop concentrations, especially with the V-1. Little was done to support him in this area.

From Rommel's analysis of the situation, he felt a landing would be attempted around the mouths of the Seine, Bresle, Arque, and Somme rivers, with a view toward gaining ports at Abbeville, Le Havre, the coast of Calvados or Cherbourg. As he saw it, there would be multiple landings, either simultaneously or in rapid succession, in this area and that the first major objective would be Paris, with a secondary objective of cutting off German troops in Britanny.

His major difficulty in this area was that there were as many opinions as to the likely landing area as there were people with fingers in the pie. The German High Command (*Oberkommando der Wehrmacht* or OKW) was sure the landings would be at the Pas de Calais, the shortest route from Britain to the continent. Although Hitler felt that Normandy would be the choice, he allowed himself to be persuaded by the OKW. Rommel, of course, did not anticipate the Mulberry's deployment and the fact that the Allies would make rapid seizure of a port a lower priority. He felt that if he could pin them down and deny them a port, he could starve the Allies for supplies and throw them back into the water. Another theory was that the Allies would land at the Scheldt Estuary, giving them access to Antwerp, a major port. Rommel discounted this because the reports he received were that

Failure to capture a port forced the Allies to bring supplies in over the beaches. Black Americans served in supply and transport units in great numbers.

the Allied shipping was being concentrated along the southern coast of England, as well as in the west of England and in Wales. A landing on the Scheldt would suggest shipping concentrations on the eastern side of England.

Rommel's ability to defend his assigned sector was made almost impossible by the lack of any central control of the forces in the area below Hitler himself. The Germans had set up a number of parallel chains of command with the result that none of the local commanders controlled everything in the area. Rommel, of course, reported directly to von Rundstedt. However, the military governors in his area re-

ported to von Rundstedt only on military matters. In every other aspect they reported to the OKW. The Navy reported to the Naval Staff in Berlin. Moreover, interservice rivalry made control of any assets which might serve more than one branch a major exercise. The Navy controlled the coastal defense artillery—as long as the enemy was not on the shore; once ashore, control shifted to the Army. But the Navy could not agree with the Army on where the coastal artillery should best be located to repel an invasion. The same problem existed with the Luftwaffe. *Luftflotte (Air Fleet) 3* had control of all air elements in France and reported directly back to

Herman Göring. The problem was that Göring, as one of Hitler's companions from the early days, had carved out a major empire. Anything having to do with air was his, including the anti-aircraft (Flak) elements, as well as the airborne divisions. To keep his hand in the military, Göring had authorized the fielding of infantry divisions out of excess Luftwaffe personnel. These, too, had a dual chain of command since they were Göring's to control but would respond to the orders of the military commander as well. When Rommel wanted to concentrate the assets of the *III Flak Corps*, which amounted to 24 batteries and were spread all over France, he could

not do it without permission from the Luftwaffe and he was unable to get that permission. There were also SS elements in the area. As with the Luftwaffe field divisions, the SS had dual loyalty. They worked within the military chain of command but always had their own SS chain running back to Heinrich Himmler, the head of the SS, the Gestapo, the Security Service (*Sicherheitsdienst* or *SD*) and many other civilian elements of the Nazi regime. Finally, any major construction work which was done was done by *Organization Todt* (OT), a civilian organization founded by Fritz Todt, another old line Nazi, which responded to military requests as it saw

Simple beach obstacles being constructed by Germans at low tide.

fit. The clarity of command and control which the Allies achieved by appointing a Supreme Commander was simply lacking in the German structure and the German efforts to prepare against an invasion suffered accordingly.

Under Rommel's command were two armies. *The Fifteenth Army*, commanded by GO Hans von Salumuth, was basically located in the Netherlands and Belgium, as well as covering the Pas de Calais. It had fifteen infantry divisions and three Luftwaffe field divisions. In France was *Seventh Army*, commanded by GO Friederich Dollmann. It had seven infantry divisions along the coast, including the *319th*, occupying the British Channel Islands off the west coast of the Cotentin Peninsula, plus two infantry divisions in the rear, later joined by two parachute divisions. In addition, but not directly part of Rommel's command, was the Panzer commander in the West, General Freiherr Geyr von Schweppenburg. Under him was *I SS Panzerkorps*, consisting of two Waffen-SS Panzer divisions, and three regular army Panzer divisions.

As noted, the Luftwaffe was under Göring's control. It was in deplorable condition. Although nominally fielding some 500 aircraft, just prior to the invasion it reported only 90 bombers and 70 fighters operational. On D-Day alone the Allies were able to put in 25,000 sorties. Moreover, the Allies had effectively gained air superiority in the spring of 1944 with the result that the Luftwaffe could not run reconnaissance flights over Britain to check on troop build up. Nor could the Luftwaffe defend occupied France against the Allied bombing raids. The result was that by D-Day, every bridge downstream of Paris, on the Seine, and Orleans on the Loire, had been destroyed. This would have an obvious impact on German ability to move troops to react to any landing.

In contrast to the stereotype of the occupying German forces, Rommel, who would have to use a lot of civilian labor to put his defenses in place, insisted that the French be well paid and that they be treated as well as the Germans. In addition, when he prepared his plans for flooding the area, he made sure that reservoirs were built so that the flooding would be done with fresh water. He was aware that after sea water was used to flood land during World War I, the land was effectively useless for a decade, due to the salt ruining the ground.

Rommel believed the Allies could get ashore wherever they wanted and felt that stopping the initial landing was unrealistic. Accordingly, he prepared a series of plans, based on various possible landing zones. He considered the possibility of landings between the Seine and Loire, Somme and Seine, north of the Somme (considered unlikely due to the terrain), south of the Loire, and on the Mediterranean, and a simultaneous landing on the Mediterranean and south of the Seine. However, all of these plans were based on a German strategic withdrawal to a more defensible line, followed by a counterattack. Hitler would not hear of it. A battle of maneuver was not to be allowed.

Regardless of that setback, Rommel pushed to have the strategic Panzer reserve moved forward, preferably to the area around Paris. It was his concern that unless they were located in that area, they would be unable to reach a number of the probable landing sites in time. This plan was approved by all concerned in the area—von Rundstedt, von Schweppenburg (commander of the Panzer troops in France) as well as his superior, Generaloberst Heinz Guderian, the Inspector General of Panzer Troops. Hitler agreed that reinforcements would be required but never took the steps necessary to move major reserves into the area.

However, Hitler did have one of his flashes of intuition and decided to move a number of strong units into the Normandy area, simply because he decided that that might be the landing area after all, despite the OKW assessment that the Pas de Calais would be the location. As a result, in the months just before the landing, the defenses were stiffened considerably. He moved *21st Panzer Division (PzDiv)* to a location to Caen, added the *91st Airlanding (LL) Division* around La Haye du Puits, as well as the *243d Infantry Division* and a number of separate units, some at full strength and full equipment. As a consequence, while Allied intelligence said they would be landing against three coastal divisions (*709, 711*, and *716 Inf Div*), there was a significant upgrading of the quality of the troops in the area.

B-26 makes low-level strike in support of Normandy landings.

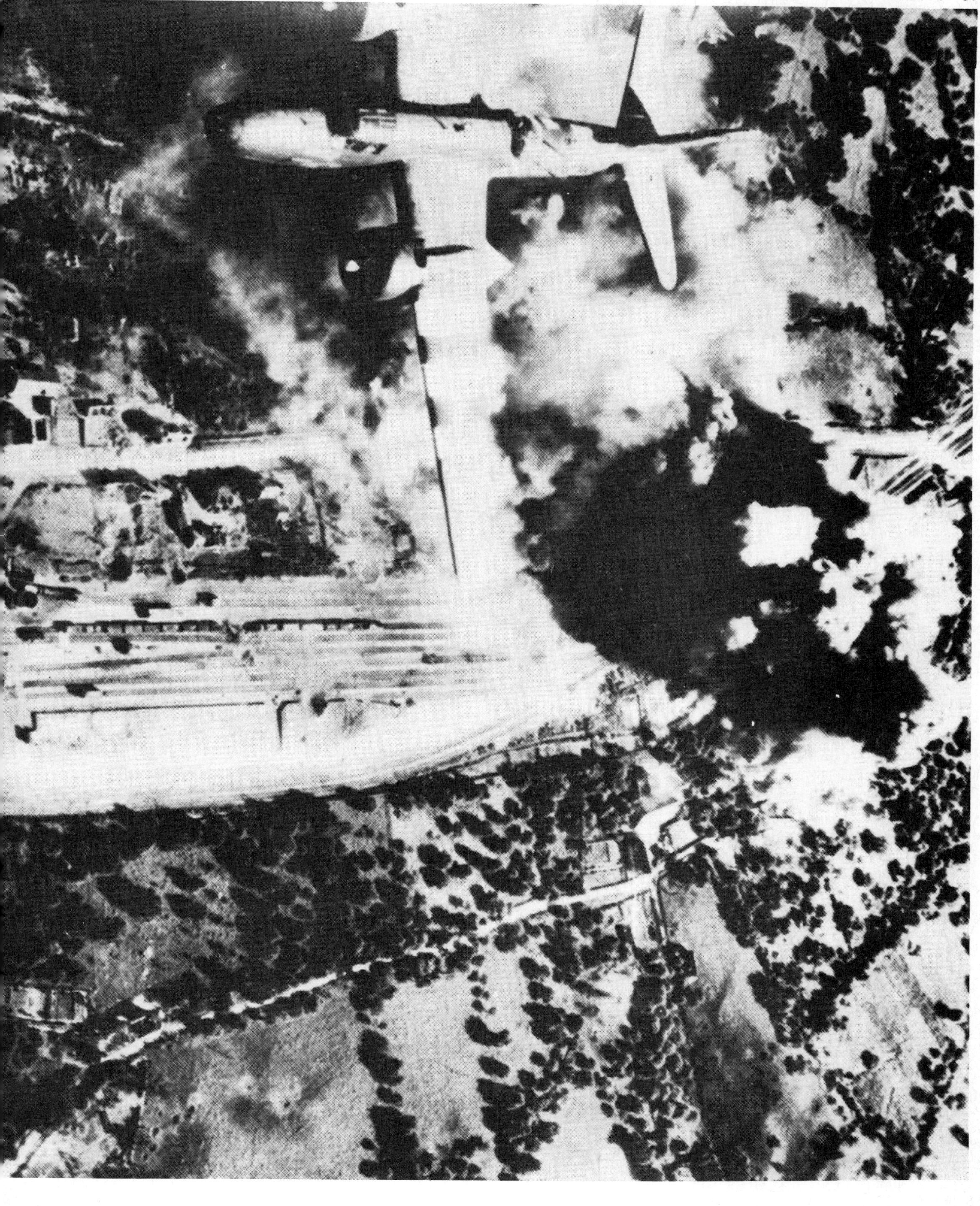

German Units:

The Germans had several types of divisions involved in the battle for Normandy. Three of them, the *Panzerdivision* (PzD) or armored division, the *Panzergrenadierdivision* (PzGD) or armored infantry division (what would now be called a mechanized infantry division) and the *Fallschirmjagerdivision* (FsJD) or parachute division, which they had invented and first used in this war. Their mainstay unit, however, was the infantry division.

Although World War II retains a popular image of the first mechanized war, in fact most of the German army was on foot. The German infantry was very much foot infantry. Most of their artillery was horse drawn, not truck or track drawn. It was the United States, more than any nation, which made maximum use of trucks and tracked vehicles.

A peculiarity of the German infantry divisions was that there were numerous differences between divisions. The Germans originally raised certain divisions in batch, each of which they called a *Welle* ["wave"]. There was no set number as to how many divisions of a given Welle might be raised. The divisions of each Welle were usually organized slightly differently from the divisions in other welles. As might be expected, the later Wellen reflected the decreasing ability of the Germans to equip and man their army. Between the Welle the differences might be slight—a few more submachine guns, a few less mortars. On the other hand, in some cases, the differences were substantial. The 15th Welle divisions had only two regiments, for example, rather than the normal three. From the Allied perspective this made it difficult to know exactly what the enemy had on hand. On the whole, infantry divisions of the line were organized alike. They had two or three infantry regiments, an artillery regiment and supporting elements, such as a recon battalion, engineer (called Pionier), and signal battalions, as well as a battalion which combined both anti-aircraft (Flak) and anti-tank (Pak) guns. Each regiment at the start of the war had three battalions, but this was later cut back to two. Each battalion, had three rifle companies and a heavy weapons company.

A special variant on this division figured heavily in the fighting in Normandy. For occupation duties the Germans saw no need to have their divisions as heavily organized or equipped. As a result, in 1941, they created what were called *Bodenstandig* divisions, often translated as "static" divisions, reflecting their lack of mobility. They usually only had two regiments, were somewhat heavier in anti-tank weapons, but lacked the horse (or other) power to move around, and generally lacked the supply elements which are normally necessary for a combat division. This lack of supply elements was for a practical consideration. Since they were basically garrison troops, they didn't have to worry about moving supplies. They could have their supplies delivered by civilian vehicles as if they were a peacetime unit in their home country. However, when the Allies invaded, they provided a very thin line of resistance since they could not readily redeploy to deal with enemy penetrations. Nor could they maneuver their artillery around to deal with specific enemy operations. Where the artillery was at the time the enemy appeared, in effect, was where it would stay until the battle was over. The *Bodenstandig* divisions constituted the largest number of the kinds of divisions the Allies faced in the early fighting.

The Germans did have several regular infantry divisions in the battle. Of these a few had been located in the Normandy area and improperly identified as being about the same kind of unit as the *Bodenstandig* divisions. As it turned out, these gave the Allies their most difficult time. The infantry divisions at Normandy were organized under the 1943 model. The major difference between the 1943 model and earlier organizations was that the regiment routinely had only two infantry battalions instead of three. They also had a Fusilier Battalion. This battalion had a motor-cycle mounted company, two regular infantry companies, and a heavy weapons company, equipped with six heavy machineguns, six 81mm mortars and four 120mm mortars. It was under direct control of the division.

The third type of infantry division encountered in Normandy didn't even belong to the army. This was the *Fallschirmjagerdivision*. Göring had won control of everything which had anything to do with the air, and that included parachutists. As a result, they were part of the Luftwaffe, although they fought under the command of the army. Although the Germans had pioneered the use of airborne troops in war, they had such a bloody victory on Crete, in 1941, that the parachutists were given only nominal training in using their parachutes and fought largely as infantry throughout the rest of the war. In fact, when the Germans wanted to use paratroopers as part of their offensive in the Ardennes in December 1944, they had a difficult time getting anyone who had actually had parachute experience. These divisions were therefore only nominally airborne. They were actually stronger, on paper, than their army counterparts. They had retained the third battalion in their regiments. They also had more artillery, having a separate battalion of heavy artillery, while the regular infantry division had three battalions of light artillery and one of medium. In addition, they had separate Flak and Pak battalions, while the regular army combined them into one battalion, keeping a company of Flak and two of Pak. By 1944, these divisions had lost that

A Menagerie of Necessity

"cream of the crop" quality which distinguished them in the assault on France in 1940. In Normandy, they fell below the regular infantry divisions in quality in terms of the units the Allies actually faced.

The Luftwaffe had a second type of division at Normandy, the *Luftwaffe field-division* or "Air Force field division". This was basically a standard infantry division in organization and was made up of people combed out of the German air force. As a whole, the *Luftwaffe field division* was decidely inferior to the *Fallschirmjagerdivision* and was also not up to par with the first line regular army infantry divisions. In Normany, the sole representative of this type of unit, the *16th LWF Division*, virtually disintegrated under the bombing which preceeded Operation Goodwood.

The Allies faced three regular army panzer divisions. These were the venerable *2d Panzerdivision*, the same unit GO Heinz Guderian, "father" of the German Panzer forces, had commanded in the occupation of Austria in 1938; *Panzer Lehr* originally drawn from Panzer school demonstration troops; and the *21st*, which was actually a new unit, organized to replace an excellent division destroyed in North Africa. There were a few people brought over from the old division to lend an air of tradition but in fact it was created out of whole cloth. A typical panzer division of the time had a panzer regiment which had two battalions, one of the PzKpfw V (Panther) and the other of the older PzKpfw IV. Each company of both tank battalions nominally had fourteen tanks. It also had two panzergrenadier (armored infantry) regiments. One was mounted in half-tracks and the other in trucks. Its artillery regiment had a mixed battalion of self-propelled artillery and two towed artillery battalions, one of light and the other of medium artillery. In addition, it had a Flak battalion, including two batteries of the famous 88mm Flak, as well as Pak battalion, two batteries of which were self-propelled and the third motorized. Likewise the engineers were organized in a mixed fashion, one company in half-tracks, the other two in trucks. Rounding out the division was an armored recon battalion (*Aufklarungs*) and a signal battalion.

But there were other panzer divisions in the area. The Waffen-SS had its own organization, uniforms, ranks, and rules. Waffen-SS units were usually known by a distinctive name. The Waffen-SS had modest beginnings, consisting of three separate regiments, basically created so that Heinrich Himmler, head of the SS, could claim that his men were doing their part. As the war progressed, the Waffen-SS grew in size and stature to the point that, by 1944, they were considered the elite of the army. Some genuinely merited that reputation—especially the panzer and most of the panzergrenadier divisions. However, they had some genuinely weak units, mostly in the Balkans. Where possible, Waffen-SS units were grouped together. It was very unusual to see a Waffen-SS corps in the area and have Waffen-SS units nearby which were not assigned to it.

Generally, the Waffen-SS panzer-division was organized like a regular army one. There were a few differences. It had a rocket artillery battalion which the regular division lacked. It had four artillery battalions instead of three—two light, one medium and one heavy. The Flak battalion had four more guns than the regular army division. It also had an assault battalion, directly under division control. Most critical, each tank company had seventeen tanks rather than the fourteen in a regular army division. It was thus a more formidable division all around.

The last type of division encountered at Normandy was the *Panzergrenadierdivision*. The German army was the first to adopt a fixed organization, at division level, which combined both tanks and infantry. The British and Americans would habitually assign separate tank battalions to their infantry divisions but only the Russians, later in the war, copied the Germans in this regard.

The typical *Panzergrenadier* division had two regiments of Panzergrenadiers, and a tank battalion rather than a regiment, but was otherwise organized much like a Panzer division.

At Normandy there were two special units, one a formal organization and the other an ad hoc unit. The formal organization was the *Schwere Panzerabteilung* or heavy panzer battalion. Attached to corps, this battalion had four companies rather than the usual three and was nominally equipped with two PzKpw IV companies and two Tiger companies, though the precise mix could vary. In the case of the *503d*, one company had the Königstiger rather than the Tiger.

The ad hoc organization was the *Kampfgruppe*. Literally a "battle group", a kampfgruppe was normally commanded by a colonel (Oberst). It could be a special element out of a normal division—a combination of tanks and infantry from a panzer division, for example, as in *Kampfgruppe Luck* from the *21st Panzerdivision*. On other occasions, it was formed when the basic division had taken such a pasting in combat that it really could not field its strength in the normal regimental organization. *Kampfgruppe Luck* was the only significant Kampfgruppe organized in Normandy but as the Allies, and especially the Americans wore down the Germans, a number of divisions were maintained as *Kampfgruppen*, perhaps totaling no more than a regiment in size, under the general control of a true division.

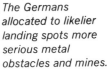

The Germans allocated to likelier landing spots more serious metal obstacles and mines.

German gun emplacement covering probable invasion beaches. Sometimes turrets of obsolete tanks were pressed into service.

German mines prepared for deployment.

The fact is that the defenses of France were largely a propaganda creation of the Reichsminister of Propaganda, Joseph Göbbels. He had repeatedly bragged about the invulnerable defenses being built along the English Channel. In fact, very little was in place when Rommel arrived. The closest anything had been done to making the so-called "Atlantic Wall" a reality was for Hitler to declare the Channel Islands of Jersey, Guernsey, and Sark, as well as the port cities of Cherbourg and Brest to be fortresses. Some few emplacements had been put in concrete but very few. and Rommel promptly set about trying to correct the situation. His first goal was to make the landings as difficult and costly as possible. He wanted to emplace two belts of mines. The first, on the beaches, would require about 20,000,000 mines to cover it at the density of twenty mines per meter for the entire length of the French coast. A second belt, inland some eight kilometers, would require another 200,000,000 mines. Whether he was right in thinking this would have stopped the Allies could never be proven as all he was able to get, by the eve of D-Day, was about 4,200,000 mines. As a result, mines had to be concentrated at the more likely areas of invasion. To make the beaches harder to land on, Rommel began to construct a series of obstacles, first at the high water line and then further down, toward the low water mark. By D-Day he had 517,000 of these obstacles in place, supplemented by 31,000 mines. In addition, he emplaced more obstacles at the most likely airborne landings sites. Given the shortage of material, Rommel did a phenomenal job. Fortunately for the Allies, it wasn't enough.

The Weather

As noted, the precise date selected for the invasion was based on the need for a full moon and a rising tide at sunrise. This meant that there was only a very small "window" available in June. Postponement of a June landing would cost the Allies at least a month.

Until the end of May, the weather was very calm in the Channel and the proposed invasion area. But as June started, the weather showed signs of deteriorating. One of the key areas the Allies had occupied early in the war, was Iceland. Iceland was Danish territory at that time and Denmark had been occupied by Germany in 1940. It was occupied to prevent Germany from taking the island. That gave the Allies a distinct edge in weather forecasting since it gave them an observation site which was not readily subject to attack, as a ship located in the Atlantic might be, and was close enough to Europe to give a fairly good advance warning of any weather changes.

The weather forecasters saw a series of depressions forming in the Atlantic. In fact, by June 3, it was noted that there were more depressions than had been seen in a like period since before the turn of the century. Eisenhower was informed that it looked like bad weather for the 4th, 5th, and probably the 6th. The problem was compounded by the fact that weather coming in off the Atlantic was notoriously hard to predict with any accuracy too far in advance. A five-day forecast usually didn't have much meaning. The task of making the final decision on the forecast to be presented to Eisenhower fell to an RAF meteorologist, Group Captain John Stagg. Stagg's difficulty was made no easier by the fact that within his group of meteorologists, there was no agreement on what the weather really would be. A number felt that the weather would by-pass the Channel or hold off so that there would be no difficulty.

Although the weather did begin to deteriorate, as Stagg had advised it would, Eisenhower decided to hold off making the final decision until June 4. As noted, missing this "window" would set back the invasion a month. Worse, some of the shipping, primarily the heavy bombardment force, the old merchant ships involved in the Mulberry breakwaters, and those convoys coming out of Wales, actually had to set sail on the 3d. The convoys made about 8 knots and needed all that time to get into position.

The meeting between Stagg and Eisenhower, on the 4th, was held at 0415 Hours and Stagg renewed his advice that the weather would be too stormy to permit a landing on the 5th. Eisenhower now had the difficult choice of postponing for at least a month or giving a 24-hour delay and hoping for better news the following morning. He chose to take a chance and issued the order to postpone for 24 hours.

As emotionally difficult as that choice must have been, there were even greater practical difficulties. The ships at sea had to be called back. If any were detected, the Germans would be put on full alert and, worse, they would be tipped to where the Allies intended to land. Instead of a 24-hour delay, the Allies might face a full month's delay as they tried to come up with a new plan to counter the reaction of the Germans to the discovery that Normandy was the target. One force of minesweepers was caught 35 miles from Normandy. Worse, one convoy of 138 transports, carrying elements of the 4th Inf. Div., scheduled to land at Utah, could not be raised by radio. Aircraft were dispatched to try to locate the convoy. This was no mean feat because the Channel was already whipped up by the winds. The message to turn back had to be delivered by dropping it, in a canister, from one of the planes onto the deck of the commodore's ship. By great fortune, the convoy turned back and the Germans did not learn there was anything afoot.

Group Captain Stagg was able to identify a gap between one storm front, which was passing through as predicted, and the next front, which was off Newfoundland. He calculated

U.S. landing craft guarded by barrage balloons off Omaha beach June 6th. Waters were relatively calm but skies show how close a call the weather was.

that this would give enough good weather between the evening of June 5 and June 6, to permit the landings to go on as planned. Beyond that, he could not be sure. He calculated, correctly, that the Germans might be lulled by the bad weather into believing that no landing was likely during the period. How much the Germans really knew of the Allied plans was always difficult to assess. But the Allies assumed the Germans suspected the actual invasion date and planned target area. Still, if they didn't get word on this break in the weather, there was a feeling that surprise could definitely be gained.

Stagg gave his appraisal at a meeting held on the evening of the 4th. Eisenhower made the decision to order the invasion to go ahead on the 6th. Just to be sure, he ordered another meeting for the morning of the 5th, to get a last-minute check.

At 0415 on the 5th, Eisenhower and his key personnel met one last time with Stagg and his RAF team. Stagg's appraisal remained unchanged. The weather looked as though it would be good enough on the 6th to permit the landings. After that, it looked as though it would deteriorate again. However, it did not appear likely to become bad enough to stop the post-invasion build up. Eisenhower then sent his confirming message, committing the invasion irrevocably to June 6.

landed as soon as winter had broken, they might hold off another year in hopes of getting as much good weather as possible. The Germans remembered what happened when they launched their invasion of Russia in late June, 1941—the Russian snows had destroyed their offensive at the gates of Moscow. A similar late start the following year had ended in snow, again, this time at Stalingrad. Still, the Germans were not totally lulled. Although the war games were to be attended by all corps and division commanders, Dollmann's Chief of Staff issued orders that no division commander was to leave for Rennes before dawn on June 6.

The same bad weather had given Rommel a chance to go to Germany in another attempt to get Hitler to put more effort into strengthening the defenses along the French Coast. He had departed on June 4 and was actually at his home when the landings began.

The weather did lull several of the division commanders into disobeying orders. Generalleutnants (GL) von Schlieber, commander of the *709th Infantry Division* and Hellmich of the *243d Infantry Division* spent the night of the 5th in Rennes and Generalmajor (GM) Falley, commander of the *91st Infantry Division,* departed for Rennes at around 0100 on the 6th.

June 5, 1944 D − 1

As has already been noted, the day before the landings was already a time of critical activity. Eisenhower had made the decision to go ahead with the landings, even though the weather was bad at the time he made it and the Channel was whipped by wind. The majority of the Allied troops involved in the landing probably never knew that there was any such moment of decision. They had already been on their ships for two days, had started for France and stopped, but were now on their way again on the strength of the decision made on the 4th to go ahead. The weather masked their movement and helped insure that surprise would be achieved.

On The German side, the *Seventh Army* commander, Dollmann, had decided to hold war games at Rennes, headquarters of *II Fallschirm (Airborne) Corps.* Set for June 6, these games specifically addressed actions to be taken in the event of Allied landings. There was a growing feeling that since the Allies had not

Interruption of obstacles by U.S. recon plane, May 1944, gives view of complete arrangement of system.

Just as the weather now conspired with the Allies to both lull the Germans and cloak their movements, fate also took a hand in other ways. The Germans were aware that an invasion was coming, sooner or later. The primary Army intelligence agency in France was Foreign Armies West *(Fremde Heeres West)*. Its more famous counterpart in the east had established a well-deserved reputation for accuracy but the western agency had no such reputation, if only because the west had been a backwater for the Germans, with very little for the intelligence personnel to do. Nonetheless, they had been working as dilligently as possible to try to learn when and where the Allies would land. As a result, *Fremde Heeres West* had information suggesting Allied landings at a number of places and on a number of dates. One of those was June, 1944, in Normandy. Because they could find nothing to make this definitive, they could not present this as a firm assessment on their part. It was felt that the invasion would have to be such a large undertaking that clear indicators would come far enough in advance to take action. There were just as many indicators that an attack would take place at the Pas De Calais. This undoubtedly further convinced the Germans that the June date was merely another rumor.

Aerial shot demonstrates traffic congestion on beaches shortly after landings had been secured.

Above: *Interesting variety of expressions on U.S. troops off Omaha beach. They have the new M1944 field jackets, but carry their bayonets on the left side of the pack, a disappearing practice.*

Left: *U.S. paratroopers prepare to emplane, 1944. Arrangement of equipment varies slightly by individual preference.*

However, the fact is that there were several quite sound reports which did get to the Germans and which were not acted upon. They had received information, apparently from someone who had access to the headquarters of Charles de Gaulle, leader of the Free French, specifically pinpointing the date. More dramatically, *Fifteenth Army's* radio intelligence section had intercepted a message at 1015, on June 5, from the BBC to the French Resistance indicating that the invasion would come within 48 hours of midnight, June 5. This was dutifully passed along to von Rundstedt's headquarters, as well as Rommel's. *Fifteenth Army* came to a state of general alert. But for reasons never discovered, this was not passed along to *Seventh Army*. As a result, the war games were still scheduled to go ahead.

The night of June 5 was a busy one. The U.S. and Royal Navies sent out their minesweepers to clear routes into the shore for the landing fleets. At 2130 the aircraft carrying the pathfinders for the 82d and 101st Airborne Divisions took off from a base at North Witham and headed for France. Their mission was to land on the proposed drop zones and set up homing devices for the aircraft bringing in the main landing force. An hour later, 822 aircraft carrying 13,000 men of the two U.S. Airborne Divisions took off and began their trip across the Channel.

C47s on the afternoon of D-Day. Black and white "invasion stripes" had recently been added to Allied aircraft to further distinguish them from the Germans.

CHAPTER II

THE LANDINGS
June 6, 1944 D-Day

For those who think historic events should begin on a dramatic note, the 6th of June, 1944 was not such an occasion. At 0015, June 6, the invasion began with the pop of a parachute opening as Capt. Frank Lillyman, leader of the pathfinders for the 101st Airborne, jumped into the night. His target was Drop Zone (DZ) A, the southernmost of the drop zones for the 101st. After him came the rest of his team, followed, in other aircraft, by pathfinders for the other drop zones, both of the 101st and the 82d. Each carried a radar beacon to help the aircraft home in on the general location, as well as lights to let the jumpmasters in the planes carrying the paratroopers know when to send their men out.

The pathfinders for the 101st generally landed off target. Capt. Lillyman's team set up about one mile north of DZ A: the DZ C team was a quarter-mile southeast of its drop zone. The DZ D team encountered enemy fire and set up a mile west of its scheduled site. Only the area designated for the gliders, Landing Zone (LZ) E was set up as planned.

As the first planes came in with the paratroopers of 502d Parachute Infantry Regiment, as well as the 377th Parachute Field Artillery, they began to encounter clouds and haze near the French coastline. Because of that, the formations they had kept over the channel began to loosen up. Worse, when the German anti-aircraft batteries opened up, the aircraft took evasive action. This created two problems. First, it took them off course. Second, the evasive action denied the paratroopers the steady jumping platform they needed. Many lost their footing in the planes, just as they were getting near the DZ's. With their heavy load of equipment, getting back on their feet was not quickly accomplished and as a result, many were late jumping. As a result, the paratroopers were scattered, some sticks as far as 20 miles from their scheduled DZ. The 2d Battalion, scheduled for DZ A, landed in DZ C, five miles to the south. The 377th was the worst scattered of them all. They were only able to assemble 50 men by the end of June 6 and could only locate one of their six 75mm pack howitzers. Consequently, the battalion could render no fire support and ended up fighting as infantrymen. The most tragic part of this was that a number of sticks dropped into the flooded areas inland of the beaches and lost people simply due to drowning because, with their heavy load of equipment, they could not get clear.

Despite being scattered, the 101st managed to scrape up enough men to do their various jobs. The commander of the 2d Battalion of the 502d, Lt. Col. Chappuis, was only able to get a dozen of his men together. His battalion's objective was a gun battery at St. Martin, several miles south of the planned DZ. Fortunately, when they got to their objective, they found it had been bombed. The 3d Battalion's objective was to secure exits 3 and 4 from Utah beach. Once again, by pulling together whoever could be found, in this case, not only men from the 3d Battalion but also some from the 501st and the 82d Airborne Division, the exits were secured by 0730. By the end of the day, they had assembled some 250 men. The 1st Battalion was luckier. Their sticks had been more concentrated in their drop and they were able to assemble about 200 men in relatively short order. Their objective was the German artillery barracks at Mésières. They reached Mésières early in the morning and began securing the town. By 0815 1st Battalion had made contact with elements of the 4th Infantry Division now ashore at Utah. Although 3d Battalion had secured the exits as directed, 4th Infantry Division had no communications with them. Neither did 1st Battalion. A patrol was sent to learn the status of 3d Battalion and the exits and, finding them secured, 4th Infantry Division was advised to begin moving inland.

The hardest fighting in 2d Battalion's sector was on the northern side, at Foucarville and Haut Fournel. For awhile, it looked as though the northern flank might not hold. However, after dark the Germans pulled out of Haut Fournel and at Foucarville the Germans suddenly surrendered. The German garrison had a

number of prisoners they had taken from the airborne divisions and the prisoners kept talking about the tremendous artillery attack due at 2230. As 2230 drew near, rather than risk getting killed in the bombardment, the Germans chose to surrender. Of course the bombardment talk was nothing but a ruse—which worked.

By 2300, elements of the 4th Infantry Division began to move through the 502d's position, heading inland. As June 6 passed into history, most of the 502d was still not assembled. They had been involved in platoon-sized actions all

In one of the most famous D-Day photographs, Eisenhower speaks with men of 101st Airborne.

day and had never really functioned as a regiment. On the other hand, the very fact of their being scattered worked in their favor. They totally disrupted the German command and control in the area with the result that the Germans became disheartened at being seemingly surrounded and isolated when in fact, as at Foucarville, they could easily have held out much longer.

The 506th Parachute Regiment, scheduled for DZ C, had similar problems to the 502d. The 1st Battalion got down in fairly good order but

Heavy loads carried by Allied paratroopers added to difficulties of night landings.

the 2d Battalion had jumped over DZ A and were mixed in with the 502d. Maj. Gen. Taylor, the division commander, jumped into DZ C himself. Taylor had never been through jump school and, probably unique among the paratroopers in his division, didn't have the five jumps necessary to qualify for jump wings. His qualifying fifth jump was June 6, 1944.

Taylor was able to assemble some sixty people by daybreak but could not communicate with the 506th. Their mission was to secure other exits for 4th Infantry Division off Utah and, not knowing where the 506th had come down (the 1st Battalion, in fact was actually about where it should have been) Taylor directed part of his small group to take Pouppeville. When they reached Pouppeville, they found it in the hands of elements of the *1058th Grenadier Regiment,* part of the *91st LL Div.* After some two hours of stiff fighting, the German defenders were killed or captured. Not long after 1100, the lead elements of 4th Infantry Division made contact. The exits off Utah were all secured by midday.

75 mm. pack howitzer loaded into U.S. glider prior to invasion.

Lesser known close-up of Eisenhower with 101st Airborne.

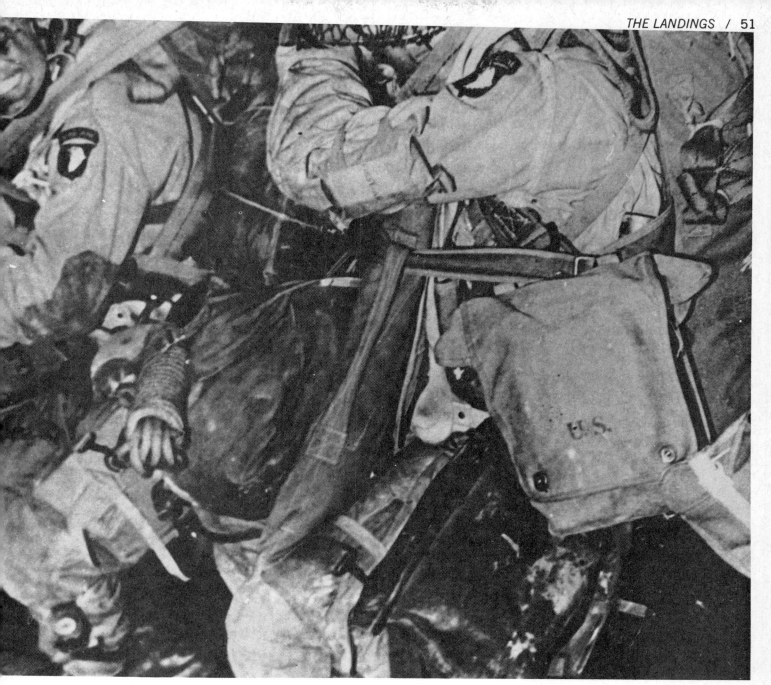

The real thing. 501st Parachute Infantry, 101st Airborne, shortly before jumping, June 6, 1944. Large pack on left hip marked "U.S." is gas mask carrier. The Allies were ready for anything.

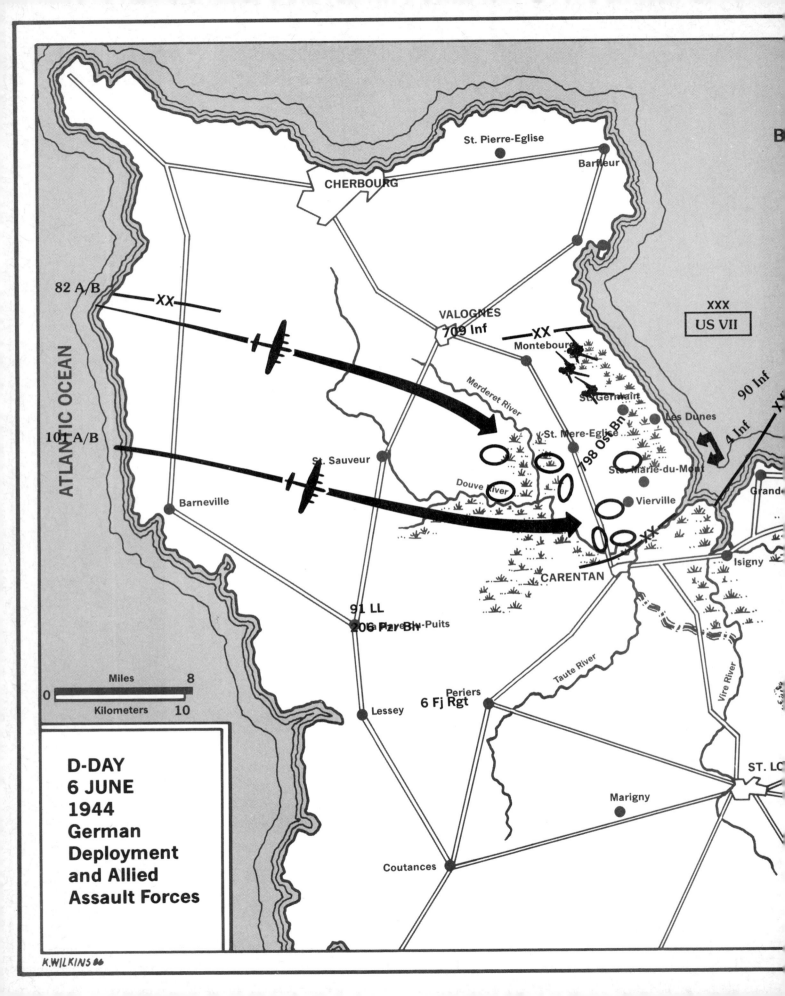

D-DAY
6 JUNE
1944
German
Deployment
and Allied
Assault Forces

K.WILKINS 86

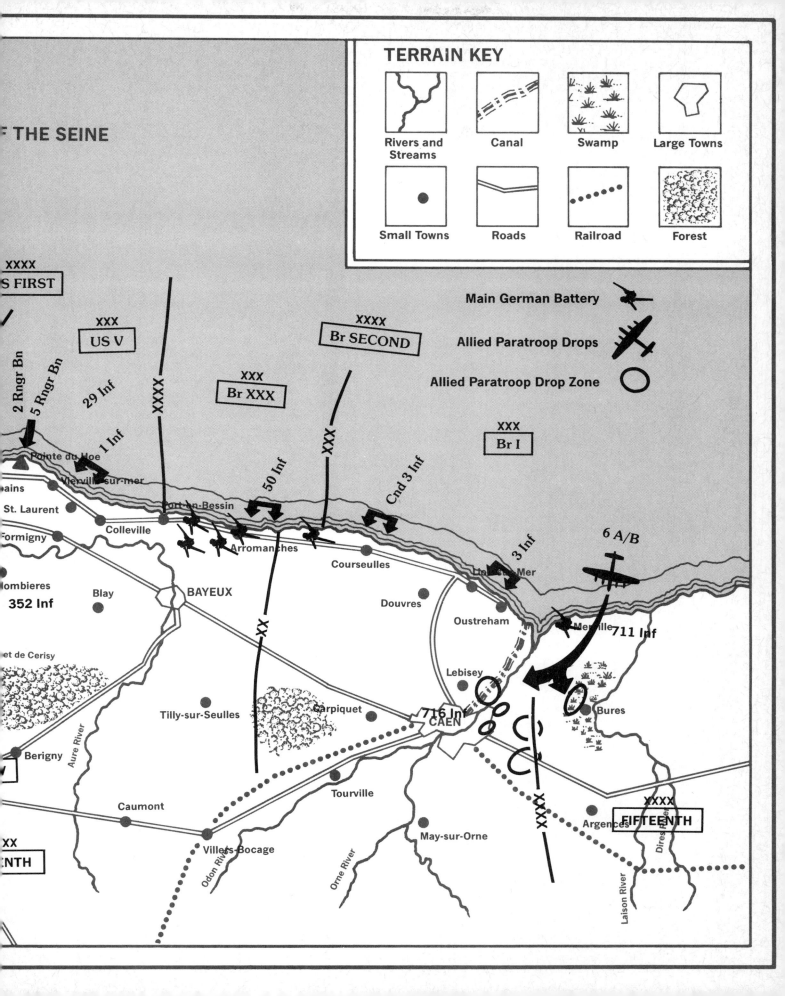

TERRAIN KEY

Rivers and Streams	Canal	Swamp	Large Towns
Small Towns	Roads	Railroad	Forest

F THE SEINE

Main German Battery

Allied Paratroop Drops

Allied Paratroop Drop Zone

XXXX
S FIRST

XXX
US V

XXXX
Br SECOND

XXX
Br XXX

XXX
Br I

2 Rngr Bn
5 Rngr Bn
29 Inf
1 Inf
XXXX

Pointe du Hoe
Vierville-sur-mer
ains
St. Laurent
Colleville
Formigny
50 Inf
Port-en-Bessin
Arromanches

Cnd 3 Inf
Courseulles
Douvres

3 Inf
Lio...Sur Mer

6 A/B

ombieres
Blay
BAYEUX
352 Inf
et de Cerisy

XX
Oustreham
Merville
711 Inf

Lebisey
716 Inf
CAEN

Tilly-sur-Seulles
Carpiquet

Bures

Berigny
Aure River
Caumont
Tourville
Odon River
Orne River
May-sur-Orne
Argences
FIFTEENTH
XXXX

Villers-Bocage
NTH

Laison River
Dires River

A Note on Sunrise

Sunrise on D-Day was at 0558. However, sunrise is actually not all that significant if the question is how much light is available at a given time. Sunrise is simply the time when the sun rises above the horizon. Before sunrise, in the period referred to as dawn, there is obviously an increasing amount of light as sunrise gets closer. Militarily, there are three times of significance in the morning, as well as at night. The first is Beginning Morning Nautical Twilight (BMNT). This is the time at which the sun is twelve degrees below the horizon. The next significant time is Beginning Morning Civil Twilight (BMCT), when the sun is six degrees below the horizon. Last comes sunrise. From BMNT on, the sky actually begins to lighten, although initially there isn't much observable difference. By the time of BMCT it becomes easy to make out objects and, of course, as sunrise approaches, it becomes quite easy to do so. Accordingly, sunrise, as such, is not an especially significant point of reference, militarily. At the other end of the day is, obviously, sunset, followed by End Evening Civil Twilight (EECT) and End Evening Nautical Twilight (EENT), which occur, again, at six and twelve degrees below the horizon, respectively. Roughly, there is about one hour between each stage. Accordingly, the landing craft, which started their loading and runs into the beach at 0500, were starting at around BMCT and landing about one-half hour after sunrise. Throughout most of their run, they were quite visible to the Germans but, correspondingly, the landing craft needed that daylight because the beaches themselves weren't marked and without some daylight they would have had no way to find their proper beaches.

The regimental headquarters of the 506th had landed near Culoville and found that it was in the middle of the *191st Artillery Regiment*—again part of the *91st LL Div.* As the day wore on, some 650 men from the 1st and 2d Battalions had assembled around the 506th's regimental headquarters. However they did very little that day, choosing to hold their position in the theory that they amounted to a blocking position screening the exits from German counterattacks.

Of the elements of the 506th, the 3d Battalion had the worst going. They were scheduled to land in DZ D and form part of the southern defensive positions for the 101st. The Germans had recognized how suitable the area was for airborne landings and drenched the drop zone with oil, and surrounded it with machineguns. The pathfinders had landed off-target but were caught in a firefight nonetheless. Those sticks of the 506th which dropped on the DZ literally came down in a killing zone.

The remainder of the southern flank of the 101st belonged to the 501st Regiment. Two battalions, the 1st and 2d, were to capture the locks at La Barquette as they were believed to control the flooding of the Douve and Merderet valleys. They were also to blow the road and railroad bridges leading from Carentan north to Cherbourg. The regimental commander, Col. Howard Johnson, was able to collect some 150 men and arrived at the locks at La Barquette before the battalion elements, finding them undefended. The 501st had landed in an area held by the *3d Battalion, 1058th Regiment* of the *91st LL* based in St. Come. Intelligence estimates had put only a platoon of Germans in St. Côme so an entire battalion was a considerable surprise. As a result, Johnson found most of the elements of his regiment heavily engaged in fighting throughout the area. However, Johnson was able to do something about the artillery fire the Germans were putting out. He was able to make contact with the U.S. cruiser, *Quincy,* off the coast. *Quincy* shelled St. Côme and Carentan, forcing the Germans to ease up the firing in order to avoid having their batteries destroyed. Nonetheless, the Germans managed to halt the advance of 2d Battalion and deny them Les Droueries and Basse Addeville. To complicate the 501st situation, in the afternoon, three battalions of *6th Fallschirmjager (Airborne) Regiment (FsR),* under command of Maj. von der Heydte, arrived to reinforce the defense. Von der Heydte's unit was one of the little surprises encountered by the Allies on landing, since it was by no means one of the over-age or unfit units which were expected to be there.

Landing Zone E was for the gliders. As noted, it was the only one where the pathfinders landed on target and set up their lights. The first group in was scheduled to be 52 Waco gliders. The first glider touched down just before 0400, in the dark. The second glider managed to wipe out all of the landing lights as it came in. Only six gliders landed on the LZ, another fifteen within half a mile, ten landed in a group near Les Forges, two miles west of the LZ and the rest were scattered to the east and west of the LZ. In all, 49 gliders touched down, bringing a load of some 150 men, 16 6-pounder anti-tank guns, a bulldozer, and a long range radio to keep the division, in Normandy, in contact with England. Almost all of the gliders were heavily damaged but there were relatively few injuries, though one of the few fatalities was the Assistant Division Commander.

The second lift, 32 Horsa gliders, came in at 2100, bringing 157 men, 40 jeeps, six guns and nineteen tons of equipment. They came under fire as they approached the LZ and again took some casualties, but essentially came down in good order.

Medal of Honor winner Lt. Col. Robert G. Cole of 502nd Parachute Infantry. His helmet is fitted with the special chin strap issued to U.S. airborne soldiers.

Typical arrangement of paratroopers in C-47 "Dakota" transport. Highly polished boots, lack of field dressing on helmet, and relaxed expressions do not suggest a combat drop.

When the nose counting was done, at the end of the day, 3,100 men in the division could be accounted for. Another 3,500 were still missing. Over a month later, 1,240 were still missing—either captured or, more often, drowned in the flooded areas or at sea.

The 82d Airborne followed the 101st out of England. First in, landing at DZ O, were 2d and 3d Battalions, 505th, as well as two guns from the 456th Parachute Artillery. Their pathfinders had landed about an hour after those of the 101st. The pilots were more accurate in locating the DZ than those flying in the 101st and of the 117 sticks which dropped, 80 landed within two miles of the DZ, 31 right on target. The 3d Battalion had the mission of capturing Ste. Mère-Eglise, a town at the junction of five roads.

Within an hour they had assembled 108 men of the battalion and set off toward the town. In fact, 30 men of the 505th had actually come down over the town. The area was controlled by elements of the *919th Grenadier Rgt.*, part of the *709th Infantry Division.* Their Flak guns were already firing on the troop carriers. In the process, an incendiary bomb set one house afire and the citizens had come out to fight the fire. Since this was a curfew violation, the Germans had troops out. The result was that the 30 men who came down in Ste. Mère-Eglise got a warm welcome indeed. However, by the time elements of the 3d Battalion arrived, about three hours after landing, the fire had died down and the Germans returned to their barracks. As a result, the town was cleared by 0500. They sent

101st Airborne troopers assemble in French village on June 8th.

word to the regimental commander, Col. Ekman, of their success but he could not be located, although the runner sent with the message did find the division commander, Ridgeway.

Because Ekman did not know whether 3d Battalion had accomplished its mission (or even whether it was a cohesive fighting unit) he directed 2d Battalion to take Ste. Mère-Eglise. The 2d Battalion's original mission was to secure Neuville and establish a road-block there. As a result, the main effort of 2d Battalion was directed toward Ste. Mère-Eglise, though one platoon was sent to Neuville. The decision to send 2d Battalion proved fortunate because at 0930 the Germans counterattacked, using two companies of Russian soldiers from the *795th Georgian Battalion* with light tanks and self-propelled guns. The Germans were driven off only with great difficulty. When 2d Battalion arrived, it took up the defense of the north side of the town.

The platoon sent to Neuville found the town undefended and took up its position as planned. When the battalion commander, Lt. Col. Vandervoort arrived to see how things were going, he brought with him a 6-pounder anti-tank gun and was just in time to see a column of troops marching toward the American positions. A Frenchman who came into the area from that direction assured Vandervoort that these were Americans bringing in German POWs. However, when tracked vehicles were spotted, Vandervoort ordered his people to open fire. The column was a company of the *1058th Grenadier Rgt* from the *91st LL Division*. The 6-pounder proved its worth in knocking out a German self-propelled gun and a PzKpfw IV tank early on. However, the superior numbers of the Germans began to tell and by mid-afternoon Vandervoort ordered the platoon to withdraw, sending another platoon over to assist them in disengaging. This new platoon effectively provided the cover so that both were ul-

C47 takes off with Horsa glider in tow. "Invasion stripes" on lower surfaces are to insure against being fired at by Allied anti-aircraft gunners.

timately able to pull back to better positions. The Germans did not follow close behind, thus conceding the area to the Allies.

The 1st Battalion of the 505th also landed in DZ 0. Its mission was to take the crossings of the Merderet River at La Fière. The first element to attempt this, Company A of the 1st Battalion, 505th, found their approach blocked short of the

bridge at a large farm, known as La Manoir. Ironically, other elements of the 82d had dropped outside their proper DZs and were in the area, each unknown to the other. One group, from the 507th Parachute Rgt, was also pinned down by fire from La Manoir. Elsewhere in the area was Brig. Gen. Gavin, the Assistant Division Commander of the 82d. He had as-

sembled a mixed group from the 507th and 508th, all of whom had missed their own DZs. But Gavin's people spent several hours trying to locate equipment before they moved off and by that time, the Germans were alerted and reacting.

Another player in the drama at the La Fière bridge was Col. Lindquist, commander of the 508th. He was among the ones who had been dropped outside his proper DZ. He planned to cross the La Fière bridge with the men from his regiment he had collected and proceed to the regimental objective, some four miles to the southwest. He arrived somewhat after 0700, learned about the presence of Company A, 1st Battalion, but instead of making contact, tried to

U.S. 501st Parachute Battalion

take the bridge on his own. Again, the fire from La Manoir proved too much and he too was pinned down.

When Gavin arrived with his group, around 0800, he was advised by the battalion commander that Company A would take the bridge within the hour. So Gavin moved on to make sure of the second crossing the division was to secure, at Chef-du-Pont.

Company A made several efforts to take the La Fière bridge, all unsuccessful and costly. It was not until after 1100 that Company A learned of Lindquist's presence. At the same time, Ridgeway arrived and directed that Lindquist assume control of everyone in the area and clear the approaches. At 1300 they finally stormed La Manoir, finding that it had only been held by a platoon of the *1057th Grenadier Rgt* from the *91st LL Division*. At that point, they were finally able

to cross the bridge and set up defensive positions in Cauquigny, on the western side.

But the Germans weren't finished. They counterattacked with elements of the *1057th Grenadier Rgt* and tanks from the *100th Panzer Ersatz Battalion*, securing the two key pieces of terrain in Cauquigny—the church and the high ground dominating the bridge, forcing the Americans to fall back to the other side. This counterattack reached its climax at 1730 when the Germans attacked on the causeway approaching the bridge and were brought to a halt by Company A, 1st Battalion, 505th. Fighting effectively stopped for the day.

The 508th Parachute Rgt was due to land on DZ N. However, the pathfinders designated for that zone had not reached the correct DZ. They set up their radar beacon and lights but were not spotted by the aircraft. Further, there was inten-

Troops demonstrate eating K rations for the cameras. The special slanting pockets on the paratroopers' jackets are clearly visible.

Brigadier General
Anthony C. McAuliffe,
of Bastogne fame, the
101st Airborne's
artillery commander
on D-Day.

The 101st Airborne Division's first commander, Major General William
C. Lee, an early advocate of airborne warfare. A heart attack kept him out of
D-Day landings.

Ste. Mère-Eglise showing road network and "bocage"
type fields resulting from medieval land tenure practices.

Typical arrangement of artillery shells in U.S. glider.

Heavily laden troops of 501st Parachute Infantry on patrol near St. Côme-du-Mont shortly after landing. The NCO on the left has the special airborne pattern M1 carbine with folding metal stock.

sive Flak. The result was a very badly scattered drop. Some few landed right on the DZ, 17 sticks out of 132. Another 46 sticks landed within two miles, but 34 were dopped east of the Merderet, in the 101st's area. Five sticks actually dropped near Cherbourg. It took four days to get the 508th back together as an effective formation.

The last drop of the 82d, for DZ T, involved the 507th Parachute Rgt. The radar beacons were just set up in time but no lights lit. A cloud bank caused part of the flight to disperse before it even reached the drop area. Ground fire caused more problems. Only three sticks of paratroopers landed in the DZ. Another fifty were within a mile, but the majority were east of the DZ in marshes along the Merderet. Because the flooding in this area had not shown up on aerial photographs, the paratroopers figured they had gone well south and were in the area of the Douve River. They, too, took a long time to pull back together as a fighting unit.

The dispersion of the 507th and 508th pro-

duced mixed results. Neither regiment attained its objectives. On the other hand, being spread over such an area, it confused the Germans as to what was going on and where. It had one curious side benefit. One stick landed near Picauville, in the vicinity of DZ N. It encountered a German staff car on the road, opened fire, and found that the now dead occupant was one GM Falley, commander of the *91st LL Div.* Falley had been en route to the war games when he heard the unusually large number of planes passing over and decided to return to his command post. The death of Falley temporarily paralyzed the division.

The village square of Ste. Mère-Eglise. Two of the strategic town's intersecting roads are visible in the upper portions of the photograph.

Command group of Airborne officers and NCOs in French cemetery, June 8th.

Waco glider on Landing Zone E. The Waco could carry a jeep, here marked with the red flag and single white star of a brigadier general, for the convenience of enemy snipers.

U.S. glider troops embark in England on June 6. Soldiers in foreground are military police. They wear obsolete M1941 trousers and windcheaters and various patterns of regular infantry footgear reflecting the glider troopers "non-elite" status prior to Normandy.

Loading up for airborne re-supply.

75mm pack howitzer used by both British and U.S. airborne artillery units.

The glider lifts were due to go to LZ O and W, landing in the last hours of daylight. The lights on LZ O weren't lit but most of the gliders got into the general area, although there were a high number of crashes due to the small fields and obstructions. They were to bring sixteen anti-tank guns and most of those were safely delivered.

The second lift, for LZ W, had medics, radio personnel, 64 jeeps and 13 6-pounder anti-tank guns. But the northern half of the LZ was still in German hands and the 505th, in Ste. Mère-Eglise, were unable to clear it or even mark any landing sites. The southern half had been cleared by two battalions of the 8th Infantry Rgt, from 4th Infantry Div, but they had decided not to head north to clear the high ground around Turqueville and Ecoqueneauville. Later, a company of the 325th Glider Infantry rode in on tanks of the 746th Tank Battalion and attempted to clear it, but without success.

An effort was made to divert the gliders to LZ O by showing yellow panels and smoke on LZ W and green panels and smoke at LZ O but the pilots didn't pick up the markings at LZ O and headed right in to LZ W. They came down in a hail of fire. In one lift of 50 glider-tug combinations, 37 of the C-47 tug aircraft were hit and two others shot down. Not all in this first wave scheduled for LZ W got there. The panels were still displayed over LZ E for the 101st's glider landings and some released their gliders over that LZ.

The last lift came in just as dark was falling. They had perhaps the most valuable cargo: the 75mm and 105mm howitzers of the 319th and 320th Field Artillery Battalions, along with 48 tons of ammunition and stores. The failing light made landings difficult and most of the gliders were destroyed. Still, fifteen of the twenty-four guns landed safely and six of the 105mm howitzers were in action the following day.

Aerial shot of Waco gliders showing their "invasion stripes" and surrounding bocage country.

Inside a Horsa glider with the 82nd's 325th Glider Infantry.

The British had a more difficult problem in their airborne drops. They knew that the *21st Panzer Div.* was in their area. They also had a sector defended by a strongly fortified battery at Merville. The British 6th Airborne Division was assigned the objective of securing the bridge over the Caen Canal and the Orne River, giving the invasion force exits from the beaches over those two bodies of water so that they could take Caen.

Perhaps the most difficult of all the landings was the one designed to capture the bridges. Maj. Gen. Gale, the division commander, had decided to play the German's game back on them and make a landing much like the one at Eben Emael, in Belgium, in 1940. He would land

a select force to secure those two key bridges, using gliders.

At 0015 on June 6, six Halifax bombers, acting as tugs, released six Horsa gliders containing six platoons of infantry for the attack on the bridges. In one of the most accurate glider landings of the invasion, they set down in an LZ 300 feet long, just as they had planned, with the lead glider smashing through the barbed wire on the bridge defenses. By 0050, they had secured the two bridges. Although the bridges had been wired for demolition, the charges were not in place.

The British had their own problems with the pathfinders sent in to mark the DZ's. One group of pathfinders, scheduled to mark DZ K, got dropped over DZ N. Since the lights they set up were coded to identify a particular unit's DZ, elements of the 8th Parachute Battalion landed on DZ N instead of K, which made the subsequent assembly and movement of 8th Parachute very difficult. At another DZ, V, the radar beacons were broken on landing, which meant that the pilots would have to find the DZ on their own.

The British chose to phase in their landings. As a result, shortly after the pathfinders came the advance parties for 5th Parachute Brigade as well as the reconnaissance groups from the 3d Parachute Bde. The commander of the 5th Bde, Brigadier Poett, came in with this advance ele-

Horsa gliders, here with RAF roundels, used by the Oxford and Bucks Light Infantry for the assault on the Orne River Bridge.

ment. Most of the advance parties got down in good order. However, DZ V produced its set of problems. In one plane, six men jumped before the green light came on and before they were over the coast, falling into the ocean and drowning. Another two aircraft had their navigational systems go out; one was delayed, the other shot down trying to find the DZ.

Shortly after the advance parties landed, a raid of 100 Lancaster bombers struck the Merville battery. As a result of the dust thrown up and the wind direction, the lights set up on the ill-starred DZ V were obscured when the main lift arrived at 0050. In addition to a parachute drop on DZ V, a lift of eleven gliders was due in with heavy equipment to support the attack on the Merville battery. Between the clouds and the dust, as well as general confusion, no gliders landed on DZ V, four landed within a mile of the DZ and another four landed in the vicinity of DZ N. Of the 71 aircraft used to lift the troops for DZ V, only seventeen were able to drop accurately on the DZ. Another eleven were within a mile and a half. Some were as far as fifteen miles away.

As already indicated, the 8th Parachute Battalion was divided between DZ N and K. On the other hand, the 5th Parachute Brigade, actually scheduled for DZ N, came down in fairly good order. A stiff wind tended to blow them to the east but this drop was probably the best drop of the entire airborne phase, in terms of concentrating the sticks. In addition, a number of canisters of 3-inch mortar ammunition, anti-tank mines and medical supplies were dropped with sufficient accuracy that by 0600 a small supply dump was in operation.

Although the 5th Bde dropped well, within the brigade there was some dispersion, especially among the 7th Parachute Battalion. It was not until an hour and a half after the drop

that 60% of the battalion had reached the rallying point. 7th Battalion had the mission of linking up with the drop which had secured the bridges. They arrived at the bridges at 0300, crossed over and secured the western approaches, capturing the small towns of Benouville and Le Port, and dug in to await the anticipated German counterattack.

The 13th Battalion had the mission of clearing the DZ, so that the gliders could come in later, and securing the town of Ranville on the south edge of the DZ. The commander used a hunting horn to rally his troops and as a result had two thirds of the battalion assembled within an hour of the drop. By 0315, one company had cleared the DZ. The remainder of the battalion moved into Ranville, driving out elements from a Panzergrenadier company, and set up the battalion command post.

The 12th Battalion had a more difficult time. The rallying signal was a whistle and a flashing red light, but the whistle was hard to hear and every time the red light was turned on it drew fire from a German machinegun position. By 0300, only about 30 men per company had reached the assembly area. One company took what they had and moved off to try to secure Le Bas-de-Ranville, the company objective.

In all, the 5th Parachute Brigade had secured all of its objectives before dawn. On the other hand, the British chose to have a major glider landing come in just at dawn to bring in the divisional headquarters as well as anti-tank guns. But there were major difficulties due to the wind picking up, as well as rain flurries. Of particular value were four 17-pounder anti-tank guns, scheduled to come in on Hamilcar gliders. One glider never got out of England because the tow rope broke. The other three landed safely and brought a much-needed piece of firepower to the British when the Germans attacked with the *21st Panzer Div.* About two-thirds of the glider lift got down safely in their Horsa gliders, the remainder had difficulties ranging from missing the lanes cleared in the German obstacles to colliding with other gliders to missing the DZ entirely.

At 0700 the naval and air bombardment of the beaches began. At the same time, the British 5th Parachute Brigade was busy moving its anti-tank guns into defensive positions and clearing their DZ for the next glider lift.

The 9th Parachute Battalion was one of the units set to attack the Merville battery. They were to land on DZ V which, as noted, seemed to breed all manner of difficulties. The recon

Horsa gliders on Landing Zone E on D-Day. The British had named the Horsa glider after an early Anglo-Saxon leader.

element which dropped in so accurately, almost got wiped out before the main body came in when the bomber raid managed to drop most of its bombs, intended for the Merville battery, south of the target and right in the area where the recon party was moving up toward the battery. The actual drops encountered their own problems. The Flak sent up at them caused a number of the paratroopers to lose their footing and as a result of the difficulty in getting up with the load they carried, parts of many sticks missed the jump time. Only a few sticks actually landed on the DZ. Some landed in the Dives marshes and others elsewhere throughout the 50 square miles which encompassed the actual locations where the 9th landed. As a result, by 0245, only some 150 had assembled. They had only a small portion of the equipment which would be needed to do the job. They had no mortars, no mine detectors, only twenty lengths of bangalore torpedoes. Since the battery had to be knocked out by 0530, to prevent it from interfering with the main landings, the few members of the 9th Battalion moved out.

The plan was modified to take into account the lack of equipment on hand. Only two gaps were to be blown in the barrier wire, using the bangalore torpedoes. As the British paratroopers got into position, they found themselves under machinegun fire from both their left and right. Taking measures to deal with the machineguns, they went ahead with the torpedoes, blew two holes in the wire, and charged through. Although the ground cratered from the bombing earlier in the morning, and on previous days, slowed their advance, they were able to reach the bunkers and, shortly after 0500, secure the battery. The 150-odd men who took part suffered about ⅓ casualties in accomplishing their mission.

Hamilcar gliders coming in for a landing.

Hotly contested section of beach with heavy concentration of shell craters.

The 9th had other missions and the survivors set off at 0600 to clear the village of Le Plein. As they got near, they were informed that both Le Plein and the nearby Hauger were occupied by an *Ost* battalion, composed of Russian soldiers led by German officers. The British assumed that this unit would be easy to push out. They got to the outskirts at 0900 but the defenders fought so vigorously that the 9th Battalion, with less than 100 effective soldiers, pulled back to a more secure position to await the scheduled arrival of the British 6th Commando battalion. In the afternoon the 6th Commando did arrive and relieved the 9th Parachute.

In the same drop with 9th Battalion was 1st Canadian Parachute Battalion. Their A Company was to cover the rear of the 9th while it attacked the Merville battery; B Company was to blow the bridge at Robehomme and C Company to blow the bridge at Varaville, as well as securing the Château de Varaville, a suspected German command post. The Canadians were also badly scattered in the drop. C Company was able to accomplish its mission by 1030, but only after stiff fighting at the Chateau. They were ultimately relieved around 1600 by elements of 6th Commando. B Company had little difficulty blowing the bridge designated as their objective and proceeded to dig in.

It was known that the area where the British 6th Airborne Division was landing was covered by the *21st Panzer Division* and so it was not surprising that the Germans made use of their armor on D-Day. The first encounter was at 0700, in the vicinity of Benouville, held by the 7th Parachute Battalion. The first German probe was by a small force which was quickly driven off by a combination of ground fire and the sound of the naval and air attack on the beaches. Although these tanks quickly departed, throughout the rest of the morning the Germans probed the village with infantry and self-propelled guns. Though they didn't launch a major attack, the self-propelled guns did force the British from the edge of the village closest to the German positions. The Germans finally occupied this part of the village at about 1100. While they were probing Benouville, the Germans also attacked Le Port, putting pressure on that side of the British position.

The British anticipated that the 1st Special Service Brigade, commanded by Lord Lovat, would relieve the paratroopers around noon. With a fine sense of history, Lovat decided that the signal of his arrival would be a bagpipe, remaining true to his Scottish ancestry and the

The Merville Battery from the air after an attack by RAF Lancasters. The Battery remained undamaged and had to be taken by infantry assault.

ancient practice of the laird having his own personal piper in battle. At around 1300, the sounds of the bagpipe were heard.

When, at 1400, the paratroopers at Benouville heard the sound of especially intense firing from the direction of Le Port, the feeling was that the Germans had made their assault, overrun the defenders, and would be heading for Benouville next. In fact what did arrive was the lead element of the 8th Royal Warwicks, part of the British 3d Division, to relieve 7th Parachute Battalion.

The 12th and 13th Parachute Battalions were given the mission of holding the villages of Le Bas de Ranville and Ranville, as well as covering the Orne bridges against attacks from the southeast—especially anticipated tank attacks from that direction, which constituted open ground and good tank country. Anti-tank guns were set up in the two towns. The 13th Battalion had five 6 pounder anti-tank guns at Ranville, as well as, at first, one 17 pounder. Later a second was set up. The remainder of the lighter anti-tank guns went to 12th Battalion at La Bas de Ranville. Actually, neither location received concentrated attacks. At Ranville there was an attempted advance by four German self-propelled guns, all of which were knocked out. In the afternoon, an infantry company made an attack which was driven off and that was the end of the action that day at Ranville. At La Bas de Ranville, the Germans moved up with a company of infantry and two self-propelled guns. Although there were some close moments, such as a jammed breach on an anti-tank gun, the self-propelled guns were knocked out easily and the infantry driven off, marking the end of the only significant action at La Bas de Ranville that day.

At 2100 the second glider lift came in. This lift brought in a substantial number of troops.

The balance of the 2d Battalion Oxfordshire and Buckinghamshire Light Infantry was to land on LZ W, to the west of the Caen Canal (six platoons of the battalion had already been landed). 1st Battalion Royal Ulster Rifles was to land at LZ N. The balance of the Airlanding Brigade, consisting of the 12th Battalion the Devonshire Regiment, as well as the 3d Anti-Tank Battery with its 17 pounder anti-tank guns and the 53d (Worcestershire Yeomanry) Airlanding Light Rgt, with 75mm pack howitzers was due in by sea the following day. The Brigade was to extend the division defenses east of the river Orne to the south, so that Longueval, St. Honorine La Chardonnerette and Escoville were included. The 12th Devons were set to take over the defense of La Bas de Ranville when they landed on June 7th.

The parachute drops, by and large, accomplished their missions. Obviously the planning took into consideration the possibility that all would not go well on the landings. The missions assigned the three airborne divisions were none of them especially demanding. In many cases battalion missions were in fact accomplished by company sized and smaller units. Moreover, they were helped by a lack of aggressive reaction by the Germans. Where, as in the American sector, they basically dropped in on German units, there was stiff resistance. However, in most cases what reactions did take place were slow in coming—late morning, typically. Additionally, they were not followed up. As a result, the airborne divisions were not only able to accomplish their primary missions of securing exits from the beaches on the American sector and across the Orne River and Caen Canal in the British sector, but also their secondary missions of screening the invasion beaches from the enemy.

On the Beaches

The airborne operations were, of course, a sideshow. The crux of the operation lay in the amphibious landings and their success. The Allies had arbitrarily divided the beaches into sectors of varying widths, assigned the standard phonetic alphabet names of the period—Able, Baker, Charlie, Dog, etc. Starting at the Vire River and working eastward, the Omaha area covered sectors Able through George. The Gold area covered How through King. Love through Nan was in the Juno area and Oboe through Roger was the Sword area, terminating at the

Orne River. On the base of the Cotentin Peninsula was the Utah area, starting with Peter on the right or northern side and ending back at the Vire with William. Some of these sectors were further subdivided and designated by colors. So, Dog was divided into Dog Green, White and Red (from west to east). Easy was only divided into two, Green and Red. Actually, the landings were designated to only a portion of the entire beach area. The Omaha landings were set for Charlie through Fox; the Utah landings on Tare and Uncle. Item through Nan were for Gold and Juno while Peter through Roger were for Sword.

British glider troopers of the Royal Ulster Rifles leaving Landing Zone N.

Sherman of 13th/18th Hussars at Landing Zone N. The "51" signifies the senior of an armored brigade's three regiments, the seahorse is the badge of the parent Armored Brigade.

By 0200, the vast armada of ships had reached the assembly area, ten miles off the coast of Normandy. A naval force of this size had never before been assembled. There were nine battleships, 23 cruisers, 104 destroyers, 71 corvettes, and some 4,000 landing ships, comprising part of a fleet totalling 6,483 vessels of all kinds. They dropped anchor and began to bring the smaller vessels alongside the transports so that the soldiers could be loaded into the boats which would carry them to the beaches. The procedure was fairly simple: the large ships dropped rope nets over the side and the soldiers climbed down into the landing craft. It was something they had practiced many times during the preceding months. This time, of course, they knew it was the real thing, not practice. But by all accounts the rough water in the channel made the process not only difficult, what with the troopships rolling at their pace and the landing craft pitching about at an entirely different rate, but turning the run into the beach into a stomach-churning event.

At 0309 German radar identified a fleet in position off Normandy and orders were issued to repel an invasion. At 0500 as the aerial bombardment began, the troops began climbing down the netting into the boats.

The Germans first opened fire when a shore battery covering Utah beach began shelling two Allied destroyers. While the Allied fleet began its shelling in earnest at 0530, the dust from the bombing and shore activity would make it unlikely to have precision targets. As a result, fire was based on map coordinates, according to strict timetables. Because a number of vessels had been late setting off, there was a period of about twelve minutes, as the landing craft were nearing the beaches, that the landing craft were without any covering fire.

The sun rose on June 6 at 0558. At 0630 the first landing craft touched down on Utah beach, carrying elements of the U.S. 8th Infantry Rgt, the first wave of the U.S. 4th Infantry Division. The invasion was on. A strong current worked in favor of the Americans, carrying their whole landing effort some 2000 meters south of the planned landing sites. As it turned out, the Germans had correctly estimated the likely landing sites but had guessed that the Americans would not land on beaches in front of the flooded areas. But that is where they came ashore, to light resistance. The pre-invasion bombardment had pinned down the elements of the *919th Grenadier Rgt* of the *709th Infantry Division* defending in the Utah sector and the defenders were so shocked by the bombardment that many surrendered upon first contact.

About thirty Sherman tanks were launched in the first wave and all but four made it ashore safely. One of the few counterattacks encountered by the Americans was mounted by the *3d Company* of the *919th Grenadier Rgt*, with a single 88mm gun, a French Renault tank, and some mortars. The tank started firing on the landing troops, only to be confronted by the DD Shermans, coming up out of the water. The Renault was soon knocked out and that pocket of German resistance shattered. The initial landings on the beach were very quickly accomplished. However, once off the beach the flooded land behind slowed the American advance to a frustrating crawl. Still, the landing was far easier than expected. Of the 23,000 men landed at Utah, only 197 casualties were taken on D-Day—fewer than in their training exercises in England. Link-up with members of the 101st Airborne was rapid. The 101st had secured four exits off the beach and the 4th Infantry had found a fifth which was unguarded. By the end of D-Day they had a beachhead six miles in depth.

Omaha was an entirely different story. It was anticipated from the start that Omaha would be difficult. The beach was narrow and behind it were high, sheer cliffs. The only way off the beach was through five draws, at Vierville-sur-mer, Les Moulins, St. Laurent, Colleville and east of Colleville, near Cabourg. Unless these draws were secure, the Omaha landings would be pinned on the beach. They didn't have the advantage, at Omaha, of the airborne landings to disrupt the defenses inland. To make matters worse, aside from the *716th Infantry Division*, a static division, there was also the much more formidable *352d Infantry Division* present at Omaha. The *352d* had

American troops prepare to land on beaches obscured by smoke of previous bombardment. 1st Division patch visible on soldier at bottom center was removed by most units going ashore.

been there for about three months but, although there had been warnings that it would be moved up closer to the beaches, American intelligence did not get a confirmation they were there until it was too close to the landing for the assaulting units to be informed. As a result, the Americans found themselves facing eight enemy battalions rather than the four originally expected.

The rough waters made launching the DD Shermans a risky operation at best and one battalion, on orders from Rear Adm. Alan Kirk, the commander of the Western Task Force, rode right to the beaches in its LCT's, unloading with no difficulty. However, others were launched some 5,000 meters off the shore. These tanks promptly foundered, with only two of the 29 DD tanks launched actually making it to the beach.

The infantry had been placed in LCVP's and at least ten of these sank even before coming under enemy fire. The landing craft carrying the 105mm howitzers, designed to give the first wave some artillery support, almost all went to the bottom in the rough waters of the channel.

The first elements ashore were the 16th RCT (Regimental Combat Team) out of the U.S. 1st Infantry Division, as well as the 116th RCT, attached to the 1st from the 29th Infantry Division. The remainder of the 29th was to be the follow-on force to the 1st. However, when the ramps dropped on the LCVP's, the troops found themselves in water up to their necks and under heavy machinegun fire from the German defenders on the cliffs. To make matters worse, the current carried companies off their intended landing beaches so that the troops found themselves facing landmarks which were totally unfamiliar and had not been shown in the intensive training they had received prior to D-Day. For those who struggled ashore under the hail of machinegun fire, being wounded virtually meant drowning as they could not get to their feet again with the heavy equipment they were carrying, typically amounting to almost 70 pounds.

Nor was the landing itself easy. German artillery tore into the landing craft, causing some to sink. The troops could not swim with all of the equipment, though they tried, and many drowned. One German artillery round hit a flamethrower tank, setting the whole boat carrying it ablaze.

The chaotic effect of the unexpected German resistance is hard to imagine. The troops, many already seasick, took to ground behind the first cover the could find, often some of the very obstacles built to deter landings. Engineers were supposed to blow the obstacles and allow the mine-clearing forces through so that the follow-on troops could get safely ashore but some 40% of the engineers were killed by German fire. The officers who tried to rally the men were forced to run from group to group, promptly becoming targets and being killed in frightening numbers. To make matters worse, nearly ¾ of the radios in the 116th RCT failed to work.

Nobody on the ships off shore had any idea what was going on. In fact, it was almost 1000 before anyone had confirmation that one soldier had set foot on Omaha. The original timetable expected them to have breached the barriers on the beaches by 0830 and be moving inland.

When he learned of the stalemate on the beaches, Maj. Gen. Huebner, commanding the U.S. 1st Infantry Division, ordered the 18th RCT in as a reinforcement but there were only enough landing craft for one battalion. The rest were to have come from boats returning from the initial landings. As a result, the rest of the regiment had to wait for the afternoon tide.

Few lanes could be cleared and the LCT's which were to bring in the second wave were simply milling about off shore and then, as they identified cleared lanes through the obstacles, began to group around those few areas, making for a sea-borne traffic jam.

U.S. Mortars in action on the beaches, June 6th.

Sherman tank comes ashore on June 9th, with disposable snorkels on exhausts in case amphibious movement was needed.

U.S. 1st Division landings, June 6th.

As Col. George Taylor, commander of the 16th Infantry Regiment aptly observed that day, "Two kinds of people are staying on this beach, the dead and those who are going to die—now let's get the hell out of here." It wasn't until around noon that men like Col. Taylor were finally able to make their influence felt and get the troops moving off the beaches. By then they had taken enough enemy fire to know that it wasn't going to get any better for waiting and to suspect that, sooner or later, they would all get killed if they didn't do something about it. Slowly, they began to make coordinated efforts. The Navy focused its attention on the defenses around the Colleville draw and the Les Moulins draw. Urged on by Brig. Gen Cota, assistant division commander of the 29th Infantry Division, as well as Col. Canham, regimental commander of the 116th, Company C of that regiment finally worked its way up to the bluffs on the west side of the Les Moulins draw.

The tanks of the U.S. 743d Tank Battalion, which were DD Shermans, had lost only five due to launching too far off shore. The remainder rode in to within 250 meters of the beach and got safely ashore, but they were late. Instead of being among the first shore, they were well behind the infantry. When they got ashore, they, too, became targets and contented themselves with drawing up behind the sea walls and simply firing at whatever targets presented themselves. They were pinned on the beach for more than twelve hours.

On the westernmost side, opposite the Viereville draw, Brig. Gen. Cota was also effective in getting troops moving. There elements of the U.S. 5th Ranger Battalion had come ashore and with much prodding from Cota were able to clear the barriers before the Vierville draw. By 1100 they had worked their way inland and secured Vierville, but they were isolated from the rest of the beachhead.

Five and one-half kilometers to the west of Omaha, three companies of the U.S. 2d Ranger Battalion had landed at Pointe du Hoc for the specific purpose of knocking out a battery of six German 155mm guns. The Rangers scaled the sheer cliffs there only to find that the guns had been removed.

In general, the 1st Infantry Division, on the eastern side of Omaha, performed better in terms of getting off the beach than the elements of the 29th which landed on the western half. This is not especially surprising since the 1st was a veteran division, having cut its teeth in combat in North Africa and Sicily while this was the first engagement for the 29th.

By 1330, a message could be sent to the ships off shore that the troops were finally moving inland. At that the task was still not made easy. Twenty-six guns were lost in efforts to land elements of five artillery battalions in the afternoon and although the 18th RCT did come ashore, there was an absence of the heavy firepower necessary to permit more aggressive advance inland. Furthermore, the troops which had struggled off the beaches ran into another problem: the hedgerows of Normandy—the bocage which would become so notorious in the weeks ahead. These were nothing more than thick hedges, grown up over the years by the French farmers to mark off their land. But to the Americans having to work through it, it seemed as though the sole purpose of the bocage was to provide cover for the Germans. It appeared that every hedgerow contained a German sharpshooter, determined to make the Americans pay a steep price for that particular patch of shrubbery.

The price of landing on Omaha was some 2,000 Americans dead, wounded and missing.

The planners anticipated in initial lodgement some 25 km wide and six to eight kilometers in depth. In fact, by dark the lodgement was nowhere more than three kilometers deep and more typically was some 1.5 km in depth. To complicate matters, the villages in the area were not completely cleared. From the American point of view, the situation at Omaha was most precarious. A determined German counterattack might, in fact, have pushed them back into the sea. The situation so concerned Montgomery that he seriously considered landing the reinforcements scheduled for Omaha on the British beaches instead. Nothing ever came of that notion but the mere fact it was discussed suggests the concern posed by the American situation.

Sword, Juno, and Gold

The British had the best of the lot in terms of the terrain assigned to them. They did not have the flooded lands inland of the beaches which faced the U.S. 4th Infantry Division at Utah and also avoided the high cliffs which bedeviled the troops landing on Omaha. Their major problem was that the city of Caen was their primary D-Day objective and around Caen the Germans had concentrated the strongest of the defenses in the Normandy area.

The British XXX Corps was responsible for Gold Beach, on the extreme west of the British sector. There the 50th (Northumbrian) Division had the lead role. It was decided that the seas were too rough to launch the DD Shermans and that they would be carried right to the beaches on their LCT's. The first troops ashore were in the flail tanks of the Westminster Dragoons. Flail tanks were another special design, like the DD Shermans. They had a rotating drum mounted on the front which literally flailed the ground with chains in order to set off mines and clear a path for the infantry. The 231st and 69th Brigades were the first wave for the 50th, followed by the 151st and 56th Brigades, the latter an independent brigade under command of the 50th Division, as was the 8th Armoured Brigade. Their objective was Bayeux. They ran into their first major opposition at Le Hamel where elements of *1st Battalion, 716th Infantry Division* held off the 1st Hampshires and 1st Dorsets for a considerable period because the German bunkers had not been knocked out by the pre-invasion shelling.

To make matters more difficult for the 50th, on their extreme right they ran into the easternmost parts of the *352d Infantry Division* which was giving the Americans so much trouble on Omaha. Despite attacking over better terrain, the British were no more successful against the *352d* than the Americans had been. Although Montgomery happily reported that D-Day closed with the 50th Division attacking Bayeux, the fact is that they ended up several kilometers short.

On Juno, the center of the British sector, the Canadian 3rd Infantry Division was given the honors. Their LCT's launched their Sherman DD tanks about 3 kilometers from shore, at around 0600. Although their orders were not to land until 0730, given the rough waters and the obvious fact that just swimming around off shore wasn't of much value, they headed in. About half of the DD's actually made it. Some were swamped by the rough waters. Others had the flotation screen shot up so badly by German machinegun fire that the bilge pumps could no longer keep them afloat. The Shermans were followed by the AVRE's (Armoured Vehicles, Royal Engineers) which carried bridging equipment to cross the anti-tank traps built on the beach.

In fact, it had been determined to officially delay the landing from 0735 to 0745 simply because the landing craft were having trouble getting in. At that there were many which were late and when they did arrive, landed right in the middle of the beach obstacles. As a result, 20 out of the first 24 landing craft were lost or damaged in the mines and steel obstacles. The artillery support, intended to come from Royal Marines using 95mm howitzers mounted in obsolete Centaur tanks, also ran into problems because the tanks got swamped coming shore. Only six of the 40 originally designated to support the 3d Canadian Division got ashore.

U.S. Divisions

There were two different types of U.S. armored division in World War II. In 1942 the army had reorganized the existing armored divisions to eliminate armored brigades. They created two command headquarters, designated Combat Command A (CCA) and B (CCB). The combat troops were organized into two tank regiments and an armored infantry regiment. The plan was that the elements of the three regiments could be reorganized as the situation dictated and controlled by the two combat commands. Each tank regiment had a recon company, maintenance company, and a service company to handle supply, plus three tank battalions. One battalion was equipped with light tanks, by this time typically, the M 5 Stuart, organized into three tank companies with seventeen tanks per company. The other two battalions were equipped with M 4 Sherman medium tanks and had a similar structure. The armored infantry regiment lacked the recon company. It had three battalions, each with three companies, and was officially equipped with half-tracks to transport the troops. Additionally, the division had an anti-tank battalion, an armored artillery brigade, with three battalions of self-propelled 105mm howitzers, plus a recon battalion and various service elements.

In 1943, the U.S. reorganized its armored divisions.

In 1943 the regiments were abolished in armored divisions. In their place were three tank battalions and three armored infantry battalions (AIB). The tank battalions had three companies of medium tanks and one company of light tanks. The AIBs were essentially organized as they were under the previous regimental organization. In addition to CCA and CCB the new division had a third combat command, designated R, for Reserve. Nominally, it was still anticipated that CCA and CCB would do the fighting but CCR was created to control those elements not required to be in the fighting. Because of its reserve role, CCR actually had a smaller staff. In reality, however, CCR came to be used much like the other combat commands and, in fact, it was elements under the control of CCR, 4th Armored Div, which first broke into Bastogne. Otherwise, the 1943 armored division was essentially the same as the 1942 model. This new pattern became the normal one for U.S. armored divisions for the balance of the war. Because the 2d and 3d Armored Divisions were already committed to action in North Africa, they were never organized under the new model, and retained the three-regiment pattern to the end of the war.

The U.S. Airborne division was officially organized into four regiments, two of which were designated Parachute Infantry Regiments and the other two Glider Infantry Regiments. The regiments were essentially the same in organization—three battalions in each with three companies per battalion. They also had two battalions of 75mm pack howitzers. In practice, however, they had unofficially been reorganized to drop one glider regiment and add a third parachute regiment. This unofficial organization was the one used by the time of the Normandy landings.

The infantry division was still organized under the regimental system, with three regiments per division. Each regiment had an anti-tank company and a cannon company, as well as three infantry battalions. Each battalion, in turn, had three infantry companies and a weapons company. The division artillery had three battalions of 105mm towed howitzers and one battalion of 155 howitzers for general support. The general support battalion also had an anti-tank company—the only integral anti-tank assets of the division. In practice, the division could be augmented by attaching a separate tank battalion and an anti-aircraft artillery battalion. In action it was rare that a pure regiment was committed. The reinforcements attached from divisional and non-divisional assets resulted in the creation of Regimental Combat Teams (RCT), usually of one infantry regiment, an artillery battalion, some engineers, and other personnel.

British Divisions

The British organization was not only used by the British themselves, but also by the Canadians and the other Commonwealth nations. In addition, all of the Allied units, staffed with refugees from overrun countries, used the British system of organization, save for the French, who used the U.S. model.

The British airborne division was organized in three brigades, two of parachute infantry and one of glider. Each brigade had three battalions. The division artillery had a battalion of 75mm howitzers and a battery of 6-pounder guns, as well as an anti-aircraft battery.

The armored division had an armored brigade and an infantry brigade. The armored brigade had three tank battalions and a mechanized infantry battalion. The tank battalion nominally had 61 cruiser tanks (typically, the MK VIII Cromwell) and eleven light tanks. The mechanized battalion was transported in half tracks. There were three battalions of regular infantry in the infantry brigade. These could keep pace with the tanks by truck transport. In addition, the division had two battalions of self-propelled, light artillery, as well as an anti-tank battalion and an anti-aircraft battalion.

The British infantry division was strictly triangular, that is, three infantry brigades, each with three battalions, plus a division artillery with three batalions of artillery, an anti-tank battalion and an anti-aircraft battalion. To reflect the need for firepower, it also had a machinegun battalion as part of the division troops.

The British went to great lengths to preserve the heritage of the units of their army, with the result that there is a confusing array of names and designations, usually reflecting regional origin of the units which, in most cases, was largely national by this stage of the war. If several units had histories deemed worthy of preservation on the active roles, but the army was being cut back in size, the two might be combined and the dual number preserved, as in 4th/7th Royal Dragoon Guards of the 8th Armoured Brigade. The two regiments which did have a number of battalions represented at Normandy were the Royal Tank Regiment (RTR) and the Parachute Regiment. For those not familiar with the British system identification of units is not helped by the practice of adding the word "regiment" at the end of the unit designation. In fact, no regiments, as the term is properly used, actually fought as such in the British Army by this time. The regiment might exist as an administrative headquarters, while each battalion went its own way. In addition, in tank units the British call company sized units "squadrons" whereas the U.S. Army as in the German Army, squadron referred to a battalion sized unit.

As might be expected, the longer regimental names were often abbreviated. When reading about the British Army in World War II, the clarity often hinges on whether the author thinks the reader is familiar with the abbreviations. If so, one just has to know that KOSB stands for King's Own Scottish Borderers.

The Germans at Juno were not as quick to fold up as on Utah. It took the Canadians three hours to take St. Aubin and at Courseulles fighting was still going on into the afternoon. The Canadian advance was helped by the practice of by-passing the pockets of resistance which the lead troops were engaging. Still, by the end of D-Day the division was 3 to 5 kilometers short of its objective, which was roughly the Bayeux-Caen road.

At Sword, the easternmost of the beaches, the British 3d Infantry Division launched their DD Shermans some 5 kilometers from the shore. Of the 40 launched, 31 made it ashore. The British had a very tidy but complex landing schedule: at H-5 minutes the DD's were to land; H-Hour the other special tanks were to come in; at H+7 the first eight LCA's were to land the first two infantry companies; at H+20 the second two companies were to land; at H+25 the beach group would land to begin control of the build-up on the beach; at H+35 bulldozers and more special tanks were to land; at H+60 nine LCT's with self-propelled guns would land and at H+90 10 LCT's with a squadron of tanks would land. In reality, the whole timetable was shot within the first half hour and subsequent landings simply piled up on the beach.

Although the landings at Sword went relatively smoothly, the Germans still put up fierce resistance in places. At La Breche they held out for three hours and cost the South Lancashires and East Yorkshires a heavy price. The British were unable to link up with the 3d Canadian on Juno. At the close of D-Day a gap of about three kilometers separated the two beaches. Moreover, their primary objective, Caen, eluded them—as it would for many days to come—thanks to a determined German resistance.

In all, though the landings failed to achieve their planned objectives, they had come through with surprisingly light casualties, except at Omaha. More critically, against all the odds, the Allies had effectively achieved surprise in that there was no serious resistance to the landings excepting Omaha, which provides a suggestion of what it might have been like on the other beaches if the Germans had not been caught by surprise. To move 59 convoys, covering some 60 miles of sea, across the Channel and, effectively, not be detected, was a major feat.

Mines and obstacles on Norman beach with resort in background.

The German Reaction

The Germans were by no means asleep at the switch. As noted earlier, *Fifteenth Army* had correctly identified the second part of the message sent to the resistance that the invasion was coming within 48 hours and had gone to full alert. *Seventh Army* had not received that message and so was not uniformly on its toes. Several of the commanders had left for the war games to be held that day. Others, however, had not. As early as 0200 GM Kraiss, commander of the *353d Infantry Division,* had put his troops on alert in reaction to reports of enemy parachute drops. Ironically, it was the dummy Titanic drop which actually precipitated the alert. However, a task force out of the *915th Infantry Rgt* of that division was sent to deal with the "paratroopers", which had "landed" some 65 kilometers from the actual beaches. The task force could not be reached to be recalled until 0900 and then had to be split to deal with both Omaha and Gold, diluting any effect their numbers might have had. Moreover, they didn't arrive in the battle area until late afternoon, by which time the Americans had gotten off the beaches at Omaha and secured a slender toehold. It is interesting to consider what might have happened at Omaha had this regiment been in place, concentrated, and launched an attack at Omaha around mid-morning. They might literally have pushed the Americans back into the sea. In the end, while returning from this wild goose chase, the task force was spotted by Allied aircraft and harassed all the way back to the beaches where word of its pending counterattack was given in sufficient time that the Allies were able to launch a spoiling attack and totally neutralize the force.

Kraiss was not the only German general to realize that a major operation was afoot. GM Max Pemsel, Chief of Staff of *Seventh Army,* used his own initiative to place the *Army* on full alert at 0215, on the strength of the reports of parachute landings, all of which suggested a major operation. At 0235, he advised GM Hans Speidel, Rommel's Chief of Staff, that he had received reports of ships' engines in the Channel, along with parachute drops. However, Speidel refused to take any action because he felt it was still unclear whether this was just routine reinforcements of the resistance or something more significant and he was not about to over-react.

Pemsel's analysis of what was about to happen was accepted by von Rundstedt. At 0415 von Rundstedt reached the conclusion that the parachute drops were, in fact, the prelude to a major landing. He ordered *12th SS-Panzer Division* and *Panzer Lehr Division* to move forward to Normandy. He then advised OKW what he had done, seeking formal approval of his actions. However, OKW initially was slow even in making a response. All of the key people were still asleep and no one seemed to appreciate the danger enough to awaken them.

Troops of British 50th Division prepare to go ashore.

The various Panzer divisions which had been held back as a strategic reserve, were alerted to move before sunup on the 6th and by 0630 they were in touch with Rommel, back in Germany, bringing him up to date on what had happened and what measures had been taken up to that time. Rommel immediately left Germany and arrived at his headquarters at La Roche Guyon by late afternoon.

The 70 bombers and 90 fighters available to Rommel from *Luftflotte III* were kept on the ground because pre-invasion bombing had so badly damaged the airfields. On this critical day, the sole Luftwaffe contribution to the defense was several sorties by a lone Bf 109.

Hitler himself was not informed about the landing until around 1000, thanks to his habit of staying up late and rising late, with firm instructions not to be disturbed while sleeping. Although some 1600 German tanks were ready to roll, OKW steadfastly refused to release the strategic reserve Panzer forces. In fact, they ordered von Rundstedt to halt *12th SS-Panzer* at Lisieux and keep *Panzer Lehr* where it was. The problem, from the OKW perspective, was that Allied movements were seen as a diversion. The intelligence appraisal furnished Hitler pointed out, quite accurately, that no units from the First U.S. Army Group, which was believed to consist of some 25 major units, nor any from British Fourth Army, had been identified among the landing units. The fact that most people in the German high command believed the Pas de Calais was to be the major landing site and that Lt. Gen. George S. Patton would lead it, coupled with the absence of any of the forces earmarked for Patton's command, made it easy to assume that this was simply a major landing to draw all of the reserves to Normandy, only to be followed in a few days by the real invasion at Calais. Even Rommel rejected the recommendation to commit the Panzer reserves when he was talking on the telephone to his headquarters around 1200 on the 6th. He was convinced, along with the rest, that the Pas de Calais would see some action.

Hitler issued the code word directing that the V-1 "buzz bombs" be launched against England, an order which he was convinced would negate any impact of the Panzers not being sent. The fact that the launch units were not ready to open fire made his directive rather meaningless.

That left the battle to the Bodenstandig, or "static" divisions on the coast, the *352d Infantry Division*, on Omaha, and the *21st Panzer*, located at Caen and, curiously, placed under the control of the *716th Infantry Division*. However, whatever GL Richter, commander of the *716th* might have wanted the *21st* to do, GM Feuchtinger, the Panzer division commander, was stuck trying to serve two masters. His tanks were considered part of the strategic reserve and therefore couldn't move until ordered by GdPzTrp Geyer von Schweppenbeurg, the commander of *Panzergruppe West*. All he could give Richter was his infantry.

Richter and Feuchtinger, to their credit, responded rapidly with what they had. At 0200 Richter had given the order to the *21st* to have its Panzergrenadiers attack immediately. In several cases this required them to abandon very good defensive positions. Ironically, to comply with the order to attack the airborne landings, which were on the east side of the Orne, the Panzer units cleared a path for the British 3d Division landing over the beaches because those defensive positions were originally on the west side of the Orne. The *2d Battalion, 192d Panzergrenadier Rgt* ran into elements of the British 7th Parachute Battalion at Benouville and was unsuccessful in clearing them out of the village.

The *22d Panzer Rgt* was finally able to get moving around 0200 and was attempting to comply with Richter's directive to attack the parachute landings on the east side of the Orne river. However, during the course of the morning, control of the *21st Panzer Division* passed directly to LXXXIV Corps and General of Artillery (GdArt) Marcks, its commander, determined (accurately, as it turned out) that the greater threat was British 3d Division. The problem was that to attack them, the *21st Panzer* had to cross to the west side of the Orne and around 1200 a major traffic problem arose and a considerable amount of time was lost, as they attempted to comply with the new orders. Because Caen was becoming crowded with debris from shelling and with fleeing civilians, the Germans decided to take their tanks around Caen, through Colombelles, and lost more time doing that.

With all of that, the Germans didn't arrive into position until between 1500 and 1600. Because of the splitting of the forces, especially the infantry, the counterattack was limited to three tank companies, totalling 60 tanks, a battalion of Panzergrenadiers, and some armored cars.

The British had had their problems and were unable to take advantage of the German slowness in reacting. The plan was for the 185th Brigade Group, composed of tanks from the Staffordshire Yeomanry, infantry of the 2d

King's Shropshire Light Infantry (KSLI), and an artillery regiment with self-propelled pieces, to charge into Caen with the infantry riding on the tanks. But the pile-up on the beaches caused the infantry to head off on foot. By the time the tanks got clear of the beach, it was late afternoon and the Germans' counterattack met the British at Bieville. In the ensuing battle, the Germans were not able to break through to the beach. On the other hand, the British were also stopped. Similar results occurred further north at Périers. Consequently, the British did not take Caen on June 6, a major thorn in the Allied side for weeks to come.

While the British and German tankers were fighting it out the German *192d Panzergrenadier Rgt* was more successful. They drove north, passing to the west of the tank battles around Bieville and Périers, and were able to prevent the Canadian 8th Brigade, landing on the east of Juno, from linking up with the British 3d Division which had landed on Sword. As a result, at the close of day, there was a gap on the order of three kilometers between the two beaches.

Almost as if in response to their counterattack efforts, the Germans were stunned by a flight of aircraft almost into their midst. In fact it was the planned glider landings for the night. Although the Germans fired into the descending gliders with everything that could be brought to bear, they achieved little.

In the afternoon, the Germans authorized the release of *12th SS-Panzer Division "Hitler Jugend."* Due to the lack of German air cover, the *12th SS* had to move under steady Allied air attacks and it was not until midnight that they closed on the battle area.

Although only Gold and Juno had linked up and although Caen wasn't taken, everyone had a feeling of optimism. The landing, in most respects, had gone far better than expected and the only shortcomings appeared to be an underestimating of the length of time it would take to advance inland.

U.S. soldier examines wrecked German Mark V "Panther" tank. Tank surfaces are covered by "Zimmerit" paste to prevent the attachment of magnetic mines.

To help the situation on Omaha, Montgomery directed that the forces on Utah alter their plan. The original idea was that they would drive straight for Cherbourg and the primary responsibility for linking the two beaches would fall to the forces ashore at Omaha. Now, Montgomery directed that the two forces aim for Carentan so that 4th Infantry Division and the follow-on forces there could assist the troops on Omaha by relieving pressure on them.

From the German perspective the situation could be viewed from two different points of view. In one sense, the Allies had not achieved any major objectives—Caen was still in German hands. They had no port for resupply and therefore, if the Germans could keep them penned in, they might starve them out. On the other hand, the Allies were ashore. That, in itself, was not very hopeful. The only significant counterattack they had launched, using *21st Panzer Division*, had been a mixed success. On Utah the German resistance had been shattered. At Omaha the landing was in trouble but the Allies were at least ashore. Worst of all, if Rommel's theory was correct and the battle had to be won on the beaches or it would be lost totally, the Germans had to realize that they were on the verge of losing it all. The Allies were beginning to bring in a steady flow of reinforcements and as long as the Panzer reserves were tied up awaiting a landing at Calais, the Allies were going to build up faster than the Germans. Any German looking at the situation with an honest eye had to believe that the next 24 to 48 hours would tell the tale and that it was entirely possible that the battle had already been lost without either side being fully aware of the fact.

CHAPTER III

SECURING THE LODGEMENT
June 7, 1944 D+1

Although the Allies were now ashore, they were well aware that they had not seen any significant reaction from the Germans. Aside from the *21st Panzer Division* and the *352d Infantry Division*, they had been fighting nothing but the static divisions. Despite that, the dawn of D+1 saw four major pockets—the British on Sword, the British-Canadian forces on Juno and Gold, and the two American beachheads on Omaha and Utah.

Montgomery was most disturbed by the inability to take Caen on the first day. Though he obviously did not know why the Germans were so slow in launching the counterattack with the *21st Panzer Division,* Montgomery was certainly aware that had British forces moved more rapidly inland, they would have beaten the Germans to the punch. Accordingly June 7 and 8 were spent trying to take Caen by direct assault.

185th Brigade of the British 3d Division attacked toward Caen through the town of Lebisey but was stopped after heavy casualties. That attack had gotten off to an ineffectual start when 2d Battalion, the Royal Warwickshire Rgt. encountered initial confusion. Only two companies reached the start line on time and though the Warwicks launched their attack on time, because of communications breakdowns, they did so without the artillery fire support they needed. The key to their attack was covering 1000 meters of open ground. Naively, the British commander, finding that the advance was apparently unopposed, committed the balance of the unit to the attack. The Germans were there, of course, and once they got within range, the Germans opened up and managed to chew up the Warwicks badly. To make matters worse, the battalion's Bren carriers and anti-tank guns, which had come by a different route, drove innocently into Lebisey Wood, thinking it had

been taken, and were also chewed up by the Germans. None of the vehicles made it back. The Warwicks were eventually rescued from their dilemma by the 1st Bn the Royal Norfolk Rgt. The 9th Brigade of the same division finally took Cambes but was stalled there.

The Germans were not simply waiting for the British to come to them. At 1500 the previous day the authorization had been given to release *I SS-Panzer Corps* to Normandy and on June 7 it took charge in the Caen area. During the night the lead elements of *12th SS-Panzer* had arrived. Drawn, primarily, from former members of the Hitler Youth, this was an excellent Panzer division, which had been raised in Belgium the previous year and then assigned to France for further training. It had not seen combat but would acquire a ferocious reputation in the summer of 1944. Once they all arrived, the plan was that "Hitler Jugend" plus the Panzer regiment of *21st Panzer* would attack out of Caen to drive the British back. In the meantime, a Kampfgruppe (combat group) under Oberst Hans Freiherr von Luck was to attack the 6th Airborne's positions east of the Orne as a spoiling attack since it was anticipated that the 6th Airborne's sector would be used by the British to stage part of their attack on Caen. The area east of the Orne gave access to some good tank country. If the British got into that ground, they would be very hard to stop. Therefore it was important to hinder any build-up east of the Orne as much as possible.

Luck's Kampfgruppe was composed of elements of the *21st Panzer Div.,* namely *125th Panzergrenadier Rgt.* and four companies of the *22d Panzer Rgt.* They were aiming for Ranville, the headquarters of the 6th Airborne. The actual attack was not especially well done. There was a lack of artillery support and the hedges and ditches made the ground well-suited for the defender. Eventually the attack was called off and the tanks pulled back. However, the psychological effect was dramatic. To the 3d Division, west of the Orne, the word got out that there had been a breakthrough by Tiger tanks and an infantry battalion.

The 9th Canadian Brigade had an even rougher time. They happened to be in the path of the attempt of Obf Kurt Meyer to split the beachhead. Nicknamed "Panzer" Meyer, he was in many ways the archetypical "Nazi" soldier in that he had a swagger and a certain over-confident arrogance which was backed up by tremendous energy in doing his job. The members of his division were generally quite young and were likewise filled with a confidence which is not based on any particular experience but just youthful elan. Composed, mostly, of the Panzer regiment of the division, Meyer's Kampfgruppe charged into the Canadians. Although they failed in their goal of driving the Canadians back into the sea or splitting the beachhead, they did throw them back some three kilometers in places, defeating the Canadian advance guard in detail.

At the same time, the second wave divisions were already coming ashore. The 51st (Highland) Division and an armored brigade were landed in 3d Canadian Infantry Division's sector to support the drive on Caen. Behind British 3d Division came 7th Armored Division and 49th (West Riding) Division. It was, of course, critical to the whole operation that these follow-on units get safely ashore. Although the Germans hindered the advance inland to the best of their ability, they were almost totally ineffective in stopping the follow-on units from landing and at that rate, it was simply a matter of time before the Allies would have all the strength they needed.

In the center of the Allied lodgement, the British 50th Division took Bayeux on the 7th, and pushed on toward Tilly-sur-Seulles, Sully and Longues. They had the best results of anyone on the eastern half of the beachead. On the other hand, they had still not linked up with the Americans on Utah.

The Americans were helped considerably by the fact that the first major reinforcements the Germans inserted were put in against the British and Canadians. In the 1st Division's sector, the 18th Regimental Combat Team (RCT) took over from the 16th and secured two bridgeheads over the Aure River. At the same time they attacked eastward to link up with the British but were unable to do so on the 7th. Likewise, the 29th Infantry Division, on the west part of Omaha, made slow progress in linking up with the Ranger battalion isolated at Pointe du Hoc.

Casualties of the 4th Division's 8th Infantry Regiment await attention June 9th.

U.S. soldiers move out. White tapes indicate areas checked for mines. Jeeps all have metal bars on front bumper to break wires the Germans strung between hedges to garotte Allied drivers.

Logistics

The question of logistics is usually overlooked in military histories. Undoubtedly the amount of beans and bullets needed to keep an army going is not a subject of overwhelming interest when trying to cover the facts behind a military event. However, an amphibious operation is, first and foremost, a logistical exercise. It is a logistical exercise first in getting the troops and equipment there, and secondly in keeping them supplied and up to strength. The story of the battle for Normandy is, ultimately, the story of the logistical victory won by the Allies—they out-supplied the Germans. The Allies were able to keep pushing the Germans with a steady flow of replacements, both personnel and equipment, to the point that the Germans had nothing left with which to hold them off.

Accomplishing this logistical feat required detailed prior planning. Once the invasion was launched, a certain amount of material and personnel had to be in the supply line if the operation was to succeed. But this had to be balanced beforehand. Too much and the situation would become unmanageable; too little and the troops would be starved out.

The military has established data on expected usage rates for everything, including personnel casualties. This allowed a projection as to how much would be needed, in all categories, to keep the pressure on the Germans. It should be noted that the data base here was fairly small and, as events proved, in some cases unreliable. Basically the operations in the Mediterranean provided the only source of comparison the COSSAC planners had. Ideally, the goal was not only to have enough available to run the war for any given day, but also a backlog to allow for either unanticipated expenditures or to take into account such problems as weather, which could and

did have a significant impact. So, particularly in the early going, part of what was delivered would go for current needs and the rest to build up the stockpile. By D+41 (July 17) the U.S. goal was to have a stockpile of fourteen days of supply in Europe. They also wanted to have five units of fire for the weapons. A "unit of fire" was a fairly arbitrary quantity of ammunition for a given weapon. For the 105mm howitzer the U.S. determined a unit of fire was 125 rounds; for the 155mm it was 75 rounds and for the 8 inch it was 50 rounds. It made a convenient figure for designating authorized expenditure rates during a given day, expressed in so many units of fire. Because it bore no particular relationship to anything, that measure was abandoned after the war.

(continued on next page)

In determining the stockpile quantity for D+41, the planners had to consider how many units were expected to be ashore and compute their anticipated expenditure rate. Table 1 shows the anticipated arrival dates and actual dates of arrival of the various divisions up to Cobra. That, plus the quantity needed to give them fourteen additional days of supply in a stockpile, determined the average daily rate of supply which was needed. In fact, it would require 26,500 tons per day.

In order to put that much ashore, the planners had to calculate where they were going to land it. The places where supplies could be landed were known. Cherbourg was the only thing approaching a real port in Normandy. There were other places where supplies could be offloaded but they were tidal, drying out completely at low water and capable of handling only vessels with a thirteen or fourteen foot draft.

At the other end, they had to deal with the problem of getting supplies across the ocean. America really was the "Great Arsenal of Democracy," as Roosevelt called it. Everything came by sea, in convoys, moving at about eight knots. The buildup was slow and had to be considered in any planning—what wasn't in Britain could not be brought across to stockpile. Table 2 shows the total number of tons of supplies shipped and received in Britain.

TABLE 1—AMERICAN DIVISION ARRIVAL DATES

Planned		Unit	Actual	
D-Day	6 Jun	1st Inf Div	D-Day	6 Jun
D-Day	6 Jun	4th Inf Div	D-Day	6 Jun
D-Day	6 Jun	29th Inf Div	D-Day	6 Jun
D-Day	6 Jun	82d Abn Div	D-Day	6 Jun
D-Day	6 Jun	101st Abn Div	D-Day	6 Jun
D +2	8 Jun	2d Inf Div	D +2	8 Jun
D +2	8 Jun	90th Ind Div	D +2	8 Jun
D +4	10 Jun	2d Armd Div	D +4	10 Jun
D +7	13 Jun	9th Inf Div	D +6	12 Jun
D +7	13 Jun	30th Inf Div	D +10	16 Jun
D +8	14 Jun	79th Inf Div	D +8	14 Jun
D +11	17 Jun	3d Armd Div	D +16	22 Jun
D +24	30 Jun	83d Inf Div	D +15	21 Jun
D +29	5 Jul	8th Inf Div	D +27	3 Jul
D +32	8 Jul	35th Inf Div	D +32	8 Jul
D +34	10 Jul	4th Armd Div	D +36	12 Jul
D +36	12 Jul	5th Inf Div	D +35	11 Jul

Note: The arrival date represents the arrival date on the continent, not the date actually committed to battle.

TABLE 2—SUPPLIES TO BRITAIN JAN–JUL 1944

Month	Tons Shipped	Tons Received	Cumulative received from Jan 42
January	982,738	886,359	8,830,149
February	1,170,235	815,948	9,646,097
March	1,370,183	1,443,248	11,089,345
April	1,637,690	1,478,651	12,567,996
May	2,003,987	1,482,294	14,050,290
June	1,815,145	1,609,569	15,585,161
July	1,912,878	2,092,771	17,047,606

Note: The tons shipped in a given month may be less than those received in the same month. Convoys which leave at the end of one month won't arrive, and be counted, until the next month.

To determine how many tons of supplies could be brought in, an estimate had to be made as to when a given port would be available to receive supplies. As noted, Cherbourg was the only real port in Normandy. It was, among other things, the home port to the luxury liner *Normandie* and while not a major commercial port, was expected to carry the largest load until the bigger ports of Belgium and the Netherlands could be opened. One of the key reasons why Britanny was a prime objective once the Americans had broken out of Normandy was the port of Brest: Table 3 shows the planned date of capture, and the planned tonnage to be landed. Table 4 shows the actual date each port became operational and the average daily discharge. As can be seen, reality was not as good as the planned figures. All of that was contingent upon the ports being captured on time and being made operational according to schedule.

In fact, that didn't occur. Grandcamp couldn't get operational until June 23 due to lack of personnel to man it; Isigny was operational a day later. St. Vaast could not be used until mid-July. St. Malo and Granville were still in enemy hands at the beginning of Cobra. Cherbourg was a wreck when captured. The result was that most of the supplies were landed at Utah and Omaha. In the first 25 days of July, 88% of the American supplies landed came in at Utah and Omaha. In fact, those beaches were used until the weather began to deteriorate in

Logistics

TABLE 3—PLANNED PORT AVAILABILITY

Port	Opening Date	Tonnage at Opening	Planned Capacity		
			D + 10	D + 30	D + 60
Omaha Beach	D-Day	3,400	9,000	6,000	5,000
Utah Beach	D-Day	1,800	4,500	4,500	4,000
Quineville Beach	D-Day	1,100	1,200	1,200	1,000
Isigny	D + 11	100	—	500	500
Cherbourg	D + 11	1,620	—	6,000	7,000
Mulberry A	D + 12	4,000	—	5,000	5,000
Grandcamp	D + 15	100	—	300	300
St. Vaast	D + 16	600	—	1,100	1,100
Barfleur	D + 20	500	—	1,000	1,000
Granville	D + 26	700	—	700	1,500
St. Malo	D + 27	900	—	900	2,500
Brest	D + 53	3,240	—	—	3,240
Quiberon Bay	D + 54	4,000	—	—	4,000
Lorient	D + 57	800	—	—	800
TOTALS			14,700	27,200	36,940

TABLE 4—ACTUAL RESULTS OF PORT OPERATIONS

Port	Opening Date	Average Daily Tonnage
Omaha Beach	D-Day	7,582
Utah Beach	D-Day	4,506
Quineville Beach	not used	
Isigny	D + 18	740
Cherbourg	D + 40(a)	13,500
Mulberry A	D + 10(b)	
Grandcamp	D + 17	675
St. Vaast	D + 33	1,172
Barfleur	D + 20	803
Granville	D + 70	1,244
St. Malo	not used(c)	
Brest	not used(c)	
Quiberon Bay	not used(c)	
Lorient	not used(c)	

(a) Cherbourg was put into operation piecemeal. It was not until September 21 (D+76) that all areas of the port were open to deep-draft ships)

(b) Although not complete, Mulberry A was used to discharge troops who were landed from an LST using the central LST pier (which portion was complete). Whatever was discharged before the storm is included in the Omaha Beach figures.

(c) The destruction of the Britanny ports was so great that after the Cherbourg experience they were never actually used for supply of the Allied efforts.

October, making it too choppy to continue their use. The beaches were used most efficiently, so that by D+24 (June 30), 80.5% of the cumulative tonnage expected to be landed by June 30 had actually been brought ashore. They were doing less well with vehicles, running at 64.5% of the total planned arrival. Troops were running at 78.1% of total planned arrival, including not only new divisions but replacements for the killed and wounded of the units already in the line.

The biggest explanation for why a higher figure was not achieved was the loss of the capacity of Mulberry A due to the storm, as well as the impact that those several days of stormy weather had in preventing even off-loading onto the beaches. They had expected to get an average of 5,000 tons a day brought in and since Mulberry A was expected to have the largest capacity, 32% of the total, between it and the two beaches, it is a tribute to the logistical personnel that they were able to reach such high percentages. Beach unloading made up considerable slack.

In addition to the supplies, up to June 30, a total of 452,460 men had been landed over the beaches. Although the figure includes a large number of troops who were not part of combat divisions— corps and higher echelon elements, supply personnel, air controllers, engineers, and all of the other people required to run the operations in the rear of the front line divisions—that was the equivalent of landing some 30 infantry divisions.

From a logistical standpoint the planning which went into Overlord was spectacular. As a result, at the key moment—when the toe-hold on Europe was the most slender—there was sufficient equipment, materiél and personnel to do the job. Once the breakout occurred, it was a different story. However, as of D+49, the American front lines were about where they had been planned to be at D+20, so they were behind schedule there. Once they broke out, they reached the D+90 line by D+79. That and subsequent operations caused some of the careful planning to come unglued. However, for the critical first month and a half, the Allied planners of COSSAC had done the impossible—they had put ashore an army right into the teeth of the enemy defenses and had kept them supplied until they could make their way inland.

U.S. paratroopers talking to farmer near Ste. Marie-du-Mont. Soldier in center has a horizontal white slash on his helmet to identify him as an NCO to those following.

Although the Germans did not send substantial reinforcements into the American sector, they were quick to make use of what was in the area. On the morning of June 7 the *Seventh Army Sturm Battalion* led an attack against Ste. Mère-Eglise. Aside from the battalion's own units, they brought along a company of the *709th Panzerjäger Battalion,* with 75mm anti-tank (PAK) guns. Although the small U.S. airborne units holding the town were no match for the attackers, because there had been a link-up with the 4th Infantry Division's elements, which had landed at Utah, the paratroopers were able to get help from the 746th Tank Battallion, attached to 4th Inf. Div. and break the German attack.

In all, however, both the U.S. 82d and 101st Airborne Divisions were stalled in their efforts to completely secure their D-Day objective. In the 82d's case they could not get a secure bridgehead across the Merderet and for the 101st it was securing the far bank of the Douve. As for the 4th Inf. Div. itself, they had run into stiff resistance trying to expand their foothold to the north.

Amidst the build-up on the beaches, the Mulberries arrived and work began to put them into place. Seen at the time as just a peculiar stop-gap until a real port could be secured, the delay in capturing Cherbourg led to the Mulberries (specifically Mulberry-B in the British area) being the main method of off-loading the supply ships and keeping operations running.

June 8, 1944 D +2

On the night of June 7–8 the 175th Inf. Rgt., drawn originally from the Maryland National Guard, part of the 29th Div., augmented by the 747th Tank Battalion, attacked toward Isigny in an effort to link up Omaha and Utah. They found only small pockets of resistance and, aided by naval gunfire, were able to secure Isigny by the end of June 8. More important, they had cut the troublesome German *352d Inf. Div.* loose from the sea and puts its flank in the air.

Yet, even as the 175th was having a relatively easy go of it, the 101st Airborne Division, given the sole task of accomplishing the link-up from the Utah side, was running into far stiffer resistance. They were facing the paratroopers of *6th Fsj Rgt,* commanded by Oberst Friedrich-August Freiherr von der Heydte, who would later lead the last German parachute jump of the war as part of the Ardennes Offensive in De-

U.S. and British tankers examine damaged Crusader tank. The Crusader was no longer in front-line service by D-Day, but many saw service as anti-aircraft platforms or artillery tractors.

cember. In addition, the *77th Infantry Division*, ordered in from Brittany by Rommel, had arrived with very little interference from Allied air. In addition to the added resistance, because so much of the area around the Douve River and Carentan Canal had been flooded, movement was often restricted to single file along causeways, further slowing any attack by the 101st. As a result, June 8 closed with Utah and Omaha still unlinked. The 4th Inf. Div. was also stalled in its efforts to secure the D-Day objectives on the north side of the Utah sector. Bradley was satisfied that the leadership was doing what it could but the Germans were putting up a determined resistance, even though the units in question were only the lightly-regarded *709th Inf. Div.* and the *91st*.

Having hammered the Canadian 9th Brigade, the Germans now turned to a new sector. This was occupied by the Canadian 7th Brigade. The Canadian armor had advanced very close to Caen on D-Day but had fallen back when it was apparent that their infantry would not catch up. Now the "Hitler Jugend" struck toward the northwest of Caen, using the PzKpfw IV and the more deadly Panther tanks, and drove the Canadians out of Bretteville l'Orgueilleuse and Putot-en-Bessin, virtually destroying the forward companies of the Regina Rifles and the Canadian Scottish. After dark, the Canadians counterattacked and recovered Putot-en-Bessin but effectively, in two successive days, the Canadian division had been driven back. On the other hand, they had not broken, nor were they pushed back into the sea, as the Germans had expected. By the same token, the Canadians, who appeared to be most in a position to attack Caen, had been pushed back and the pressure relieved for the time being.

The previous day, in order to focus the operation more narrowly for each major command headquarters, von Schweppenburg's Panzergruppe West was brought up from Paris to take charge in the sector between the Orne and Tilly-sur-Seulles. However, it was not until the evening of June 8 that the headquarters was in place and ready to take over.

In one of the fortunes of war, June 8 saw three pieces of critical intelligence fall into German hands. They were able to get a copy of the Beachmaster's copy of the VII Corps landing plans on Utah, which not only gave a detailed timetable for landings on Utah, but also informed the Beachmaster about general plans for Omaha and XXX Corps area of Gold and Juno. This was followed by the discovery of the V

Corps plans on a dead American in the Omaha sector. Further, the Germans got a signal procedure book listing cover names for various pieces of terrain and German defenses, as well as, from a separate source, a British map of those defenses. Since the Allies continued to use those cover names for some days to come, it gave the Germans who were listening to their signals an edge.

Von Rundstedt was now convinced that this was, indeed, the major invasion and should be treated as such.

In 50th Division's sector, Montgomery landed on June 8 and set up his command post in Creuilly. With his typical caution, Montgomery decided that a direct assault on Caen was not practical. Instead, effort was to be devoted to consolidating positions and working around to the west, generally in the direction of Villers-Bocage and Evrecy.

One problem which was becoming evident in the British sector, and was to bother them more in the days to come, was the lack of transportation for the infantry. During this period there was little opportunity for sleep. Not only was fatigue becoming a real problem, but it was made worse by the fact that the infantry had to walk everywhere they went. As a result, there seemed to be less of a sense of urgency than, for example, was displayed by the German divisions on the scene.

In England deception plans were still going on. On June 8 messages were sent to the Resistance groups calling upon them to begin sabotage throughout northern France and Belgium. However, to continue the ruse, the Allies stepped up the activities of Patton's fictitious "First U.S. Army Group" and made a point of directing a number of messages at Resistance groups in the Pas de Calais. Because the Germans were so heavily concentrated in that area, in fact there were not many Resistance groups at all. However, the effort was made to make it seem as though there were many and the net effect of all of this is that Fremde Heeres West declared that in all probability the Allies would be making a major landing in the Pas de Calais around June 10.

Ultra: The "Secret" Victory

There seems to be a cycle in the writing of the history of a war in which the participants on each side write their memoirs first and later a second wave of writers comes along, examines what the participants said happened plus what the official records show, and often draw other conclusions. From this approach came the information that Napoleon suffered from various ailments at Waterloo and it was this which cost him his chance for victory, not the low level of training of his troops and the absence of so many of the key marshalls who had won battles for him before. There seems to be a constant search for the "true" piece of insight which will explain away all confusion in writing about a battle.

In World War II this same kind of work went on—and still does. However, after almost thirty years following the end of the war, the idea that there were any great revelations to be made did not seem very sensible. Then a book entitled *The Ultra Secret* was written by Frederick W. Winterbotham, the essence of which was that the Allies, especially the British, were reading the key transmissions of the German high command and that a number of the key events of the war turned, not on the great intuition of the commanders but on the cold knowledge of what the Germans intended to do.

The key to this was an encrypting machine which had been smuggled out of Poland to Britain just before the war. The British called the machine "Enigma" and gave the whole project the name "Ultra," which was the term used for the highest level of intelligence derived from cryptanalysis. The Enigma machine was the key to the entire system. It consisted of several wheels which would be set in a specific order and which would then encrypt (or decrypt) messages. The manner in which the wheels were set determined the actual code to be involved. Of

course, just to preclude a set of code instructions falling into enemy hands, these would be changed periodically. When that was done, then, in the absence of a new set of books, it was strictly an exercise in random search to find out the new way in which the wheels would be set when they were changed. What Ultra did was come up with a machine which would examine all of the Enigma messages received from monitoring German signals and then, based on a knowledge of how the Enigma machine was set up, would, in effect, calculate how the wheels were to be set for that particular period. In fact, this device, which was nicknamed "The Bomb" actually decrypted the message directly. Beneficial to the Allied cause was the fact that the Germans had high confidence in this system and didn't change the coding too often.

It should be emphasized that Ultra didn't mean that the Allies read every signal that the Germans sent. First, there were the periods when the Germans changed the configuration of the wheels, while the new arrangement was worked out. All signals in that period could be recorded for future decryption but if there had to be an immediate reaction, during that period there was nothing which could be done. Second, the Enigma was only used by the higher level units. Lower level units did not use Enigma at all but had different systems. Third, from time to time the Germans simply would not trust the radio at all to send critical messages but would rely on messengers instead. Land lines—telephone and telegraph—might also be used. One of the key reasons why the Germans achieved such surprise in the Battle of the Bulge was that they were not sending the key messages, which would have tipped the Allies off, over the radio at all. They were being hand-carried for secrecy purposes.

Nonetheless, Ultra proved invaluable during this period. First, it eased concerns by intercepting messages which indicated that the Germans had accepted the ruse of Fortitude South— that the main landing was in the Pas de Calais. Likewise, on the eve of D-Day they obtained the offical Luftwaffe weather report, which predicted that the bad weather which had moved the landing back a day, would actually continue for some period of time. It was in reliance on this that the Germans let down their guard and decided to have their war games, as well as allowing Rommel to believe it was a safe time to go back to Germany and try to get more support from Hitler. Knowing that the Germans did not anticipate the critical break in the weather which actually permitted the landings allowed the Allies to proceed with greater confidence that they would have surprise. Ultra continued to monitor the German signals and was therefore able to keep the Allies informed that the Germans were being very reluctant to commit their reserves and that, in fact, they were still buying the Fortitude South ruse.

Ultra did not, by itself, tip the scales of war in favor of the Allies but, by contrast, when the troops landed in Normandy, there was not a total fog on the Allied side as to what to expect. They had a good idea what the Germans had and that they could overcome it.

June 9, 1944 D +3

With the failure to push the British back into the sea, the Germans gradually withdrew the forces holding the gap between Sword and Juno beaches in order to form a shield around Caen. On the evening of June 9 the German strength was augmented by the arrival of *Panzer Lehr Div.* This was the strongest Panzer division in the entire German army, not excepting the Waffen-SS divisions. Originally formed from the German armor school, it was decidedly better equipped than the other Panzer units. Not only

did *Panzer Lehr* have Panther tanks, but also the more powerful Tiger tanks. It has been located at Chartres when the release order came and had moved under heavy Allied air attacks, losing five tanks and 84 self-propelled guns and other vehicles in the move. They were put in on the left flank of "Hitler Jugend" and assigned the defense of Tilly-sur-Seulles, an objective of British 50th Division.

Rommel decided that a determined strike from Panzergruppe West on the night of June 10–11 would be critical to his plan to push the Allies off the beaches but before the planning was completed, there was a devastating raid

German POWs carry American wounded. The two Germans on the right wear the characteristic camouflaged paratroopers' smock.

9th Division mortar-men on July 27th, wearing the coveralls sometimes favored by artillerymen and tank crews. Bocage in background greatly limit visibility.

right on the Panzergruppe headquarters which virtually wiped it out, killing the Chief of Staff and the operations officer, among others. Von Schweppenburg himself was injured and it was not until June 26 that they were back in business with an improvised staff. Best estimates were that the Panzergruppe was careless about its radio transmissions and, once identified by the Allies, was targeted accordingly.

Although bad weather on June 9 and 10 impaired Allied air operations, because of setbacks such as this, the Germans were unable to take advantage of that situation.

In the American sectors, progress was very slow out of the V Corps area simply due to the bocage. There were few long range engagements. Everything seemed point blank, from one hedgerow to another. This terrain was ideally suited for the defenders since a very weak unit could hold off a strong one in the hedgerows of Normandy. By midday, the U.S. was able to have 2d Infantry Division, which had originally landed on June 7, become operational in the V Corps area, between the 29th Infantry Division and the 1st. The 2d was as-

signed the objective of taking the Forêt de Cerisy, which constituted high ground and also dominated the Omaha beachhead. It was seen as a potential assembly area of German counterattacks. Based on the progress through the bocage up to that point, it was anticipated that this would take a number of days to accomplish. However, even if it did, pressure against the Germans in that sector would preclude the Germans from mounting a counterattack since they would be too busy contending with the 2d's attacks.

A similar problem faced the troops on Utah in their efforts to push west or south for the link-up. The 4th Inf. Div., which was trying to advance to the north, had a somewhat different problem in that the defenders were on the higher ground and had established themselves in strong positions. As a result, they were making little headway toward gaining their D-Day objectives in that area. The situation was made more difficult by the arrival of a new division, the *346th Infantry*, during this period, which allowed the Germans to narrow the front held by the defending divisions already in place.

C-47s, the "workhorse" of the U.S. Airborne effort.

In a pre-invasion light moment, private paints soldiers' home towns on helmets. Each helmet also has the "ivy" of the 4th Division.

THE NORMANDY CAMPAIGN

A Color Portfolio

U.S. Army soldiers march through an English coastal town, en route to board landing ships for the Normandy invasion.

U.S. Army paratrooper, Cpl. Louis E. Laird of the 101st Airborne Division smiles as he boards a C-47 transport plane. He carries his "bazooka" anti-tank rocket launcher with him.
U.S. ARMY

After loading their equipment, U.S. Army troops of the 1st Infantry Division pose for the camera.
U.S. ARMY

U.S. Army Rangers share a pack of "Lucky Strike" cigarettes prior to the invasion.
U.S. ARMY

A U.S. Navy LCT nicknamed "Channel Fever" waits in an English port for the invasion signal, with its load of Army troops and vehicles on board.
U.S. ARMY

American troops crowd into landing craft for transportation during pre-invasion loading in an English port. The craft in the foreground are British landing and assault craft, LCAs. In the background are the USS LCI-87, LCI-84, and the LCI-497, which was lost on the first day of the invasion.
U.S. ARMY

U.S. Army troops board an LCV landing craft in an English port, as barrage balloons are prepared in the background.
U.S. ARMY

The USS LCT-624 *and* LCT-85 *unload. The* LCI-85 *was lost later during the Normady invasion.*

U.S. COAST GUARD

Beachmaster uses walkie-talkie radio to maintain contact with other sections of his beach battalion. Other communications men stand ready to use signal lamp and flags, while one unfortunate soldier digs the foxhole.

NATIONAL ARCHIVES

Corpsmen of a Navy Battalion's medical section "operate" on the beach.

NATIONAL ARCHIVES

Army troops and equipment unload from the LCT-201.
Vehicles include a half-track truck, and Sherman tank with
flotation skirts.

An Army M-4 Sherman tank with bulldozer blade attachment unloads.

U.S. COAST GUARD

ABOVE AND BELOW:

USS LCT-149 *and* LCT-495 *beached and unloading.*

NATIONAL ARCHIVES

The HMS Prince Baudouin *launch three LCAs filled with American troops.*

The USS LST-289 *arrives in Dartmouth harbor, England after being torpedoed by German MTBs.*

CLOCKWISE:

A truck boards the USS LST-47 during loading operations. A LCM is at right.
NATIONAL ARCHIVES

The USS LST-49 loads an Army tank with a towed field gun at an English port.
NATIONAL ARCHIVES

Army half-track anti-aircraft machine gun backs into the well deck of a Navy LCT during pre-invasion loading.
U.S. ARMY

Army M-4 Sherman tanks and other equipment is loaded onto a Navy LCT.
U.S. ARMY

ABOVE AND RIGHT:

British landing craft churn through the waters, carrying American troops.

From a hilltop overlooking the road into St. Lo, two French boys watch convoys of Allied vehicles pass through the badly damaged city, en route to the front. St. Lo was the scene of major fighting during the latter stages of the Normandy campaign.

Two nuns and a French family examine the ruins of the bombed church of St. Malo, in Valognes. The town was badly battered during the drive on Cherbourg.
U.S. ARMY

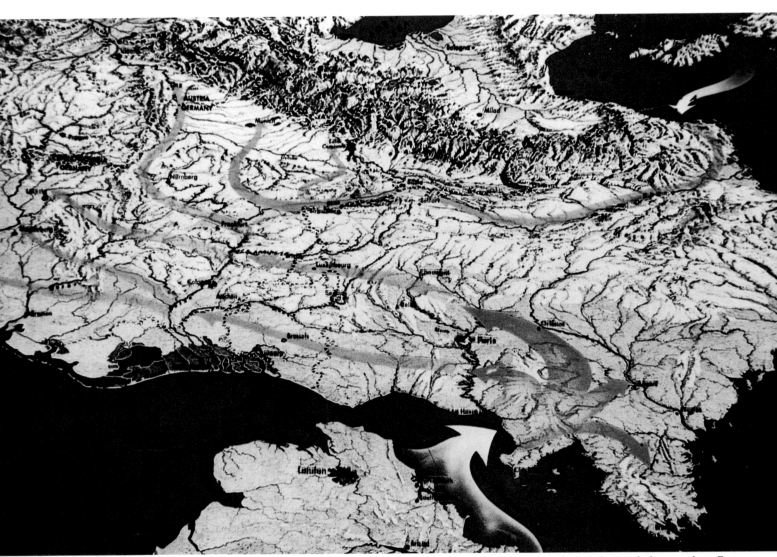

This map shows the lines of attack against Germany, beginning with the Normandy invasions and, then, southern France. The map is reproduced from the Biennial Report, 1944-1945, *of Army Chief of Staff George C. Marshall to the Secretary of War. The map looks south.*

U.S. ARMY

The 1st Divisions' 33rd Field Artillery brings ashore a 105mm howitzer.

C47 down in the channel, June 6.

Bocage

Much is made of the hedgerows of Normandy, the bocage. The problem of putting a border around farm lands has always existed. In some areas, where glaciers had left a lot of rocks, stone walls were common. In other areas, wooden fences were the rule. In Normandy, the farmers had put up hedges to border their farms.

However, these were not the ordinary hedges of the kind found in people's front yards. These had deep ditches running along them and had been in place so long that their roots ran deep and they were very thick. A tank can uproot a small tree. But tanks running into the bocage found that they could not penetrate the hedges. More typically, they would ride up on the hedges, which would bend but not break under the tank's weight. The tank would ride on it and, like as not, find itself hung up on the hedge, the growth actually holding the tank off the ground, with its tracks unable to get enough of a purchase to either back off or move ahead, and with their thin belly armor now presented to enemy fire.

One could fire through the hedges but not move through them.

The solution was devised by two members of the American 102d Mechanized Cavalry Squadron, originally part of the New Jersey National Guard. Named after one of the inventors, Sergeant Cullin, the solution was to weld a series of steel teeth or prongs to a bracket which would then be mounted on a tank. The prototype was made from pieces of the German anti-tank defenses. This device would cut into the hedges and clear a path for the tank. While the Cullin Hedgerow Device didn't make the hedgerows disappear, it did ensure that they were not the obstacle they once were.

U.S. Infantry move through typical Normandy bocage country.

While no one was evoking the name of Gallipoli at this point, the fact is that the battle had come to a complete halt and began to take on the look of position warfare. Gains were measured in hundreds of meters, with neither side seeming to be able to secure the upper hand. The Allies were putting troops ashore as rapidly as possible while the Germans were slow about committing their reinforcements because the deception plans had gone so well. From the Allied point of view, this delay was critical. If the Germans were able to bring up enough troops, they might solidify the line so well that additional Allied units would simply run out of room to maneuver and get in each other's way. On the other hand, from the German point of view, they had to realize that once this maneuver room was obtained, the Allies would be able to call upon their superior numbers and eventually break out.

June 10, 1944 D + 4

In anticipation of an Allied landing in France, Hitler had designated several key cities as "fortresses," although nothing much was done about fortifying them against land attacks. Cherbourg was one such city. When it became apparent that Cherbourg was a major Allied goal, the Germans were compelled to set troops aside for the defense of the "fortress." In this case, the *77th, 91st, 247th* and *709th Infantry Divisions* were designated for the defense of Cherbourg. This influenced the course of the battle since it pre-determined the direction in which they might withdraw if they were pushed out of their present positions. They had to cover Cherbourg, rather than withdraw toward the south in an attempt to seal off the base of the peninsula.

The 101st, having carefully picked its way across the causeways through the flooded Douve River valley, finally made contact between its 327th Glider Infantry and the 175th Inf. Rgt. of the 29th Division, which had crossed the Vire River west of Isigny. The two American beaches were finally linked. At that time, the contacts were not all that firm. That would require a few more days of fighting to allow the kind of link really needed.

In contrast to the general slow going in the U.S. areas, when the 2d Inf. Div. jumped off in its attack to secure the Forêt de Cerisy, they found very little opposition and by late in the day, had actually crossed through the forest, encountering only light opposition. On the east side of the 2d, the 1st Inf. Div. found similar light opposition and proceeded to advance on the hill of Caumont, which was an even more dominant piece of terrain than the Forêt de Cerisy. Actually, what had happened was that the Americans were now gaining the benefit of earlier operations against the stubborn German *352d Inf. Div.*, during the course of which they had broken loose both the east and west flanks of that division from both other German units and any solid terrain feature, such as the sea. The *352d* was actually being pulled out on the evening of 9–10 June toward the Elle River, in front of St. Lô.

U.S. Sherman passes knocked out German Mark IVs, July 9th.

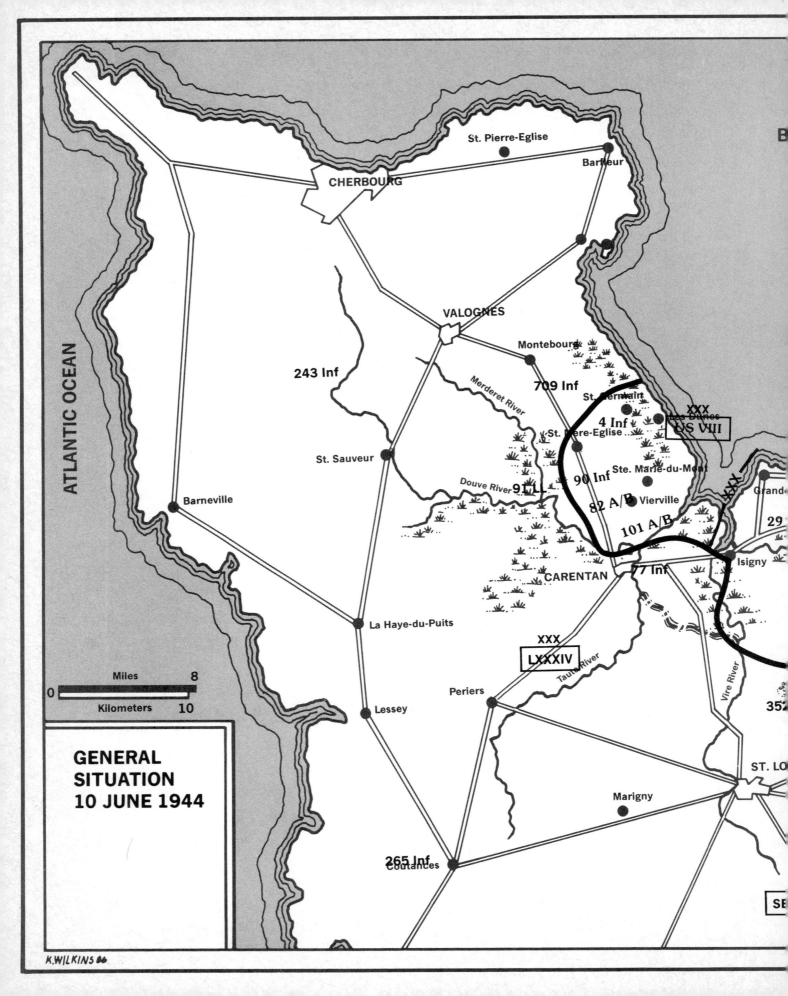

St. Pierre-Eglise

Barfleur

CHERBOURG

VALOGNES

Montebourg

ATLANTIC OCEAN

243 Inf

709 Inf

St. Germain

4 Inf

les Dunes

St. Sauveur

St. Pere-Eglise

XXX
US VIII

Merderet River

Ste. Marie-du-Mont

90 Inf

Grande

Barneville

Douve River

91 LL

82 A/B

Vierville

29

101 A/B

Isigny

CARENTAN

77 Inf

La Haye-du-Puits

XXX
LXXXIV

Taute River

Vire River

352

Miles 8

0

Periers

Kilometers 10

Lessey

**GENERAL
SITUATION
10 JUNE 1944**

ST. LO

Marigny

265 Inf

Coutances

SE

K.WILKINS 86

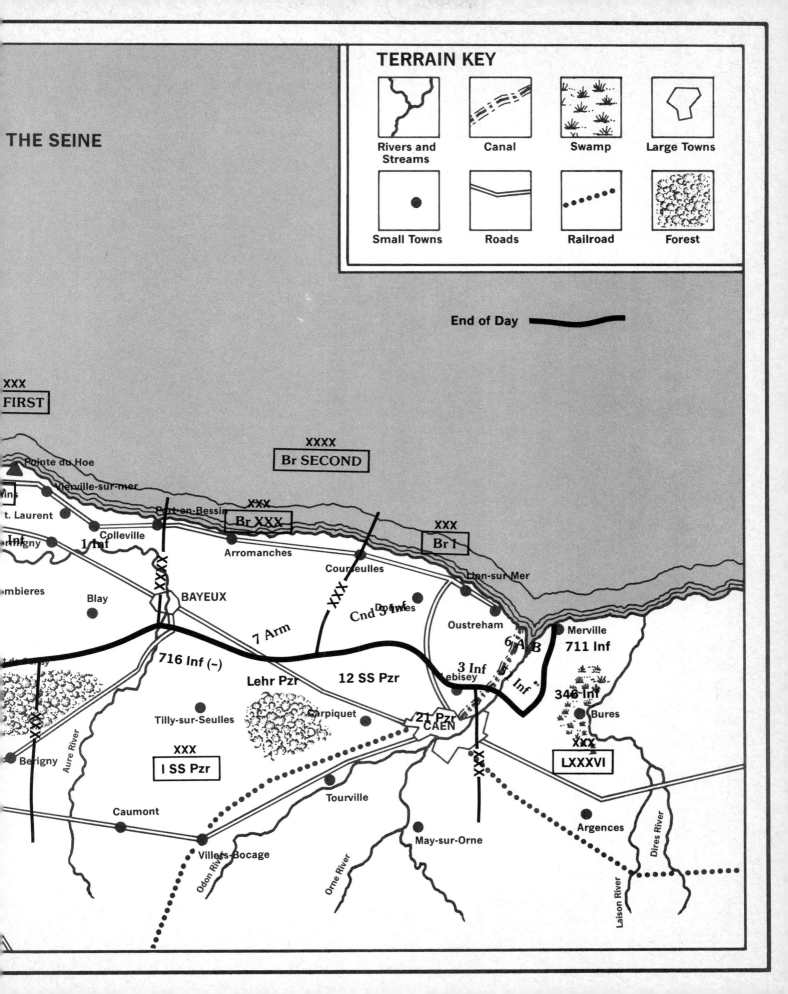

THE SEINE

TERRAIN KEY

Rivers and Streams	Canal	Swamp	Large Towns
Small Towns	Roads	Railroad	Forest

End of Day

XXX
FIRST

XXXX
Br SECOND

Pointe du Hoe

Vierville-sur-mer

ins

t. Laurent

Port-en-Bessin

XXX
Br XXX

XXX
Br I

Inf

1 Inf

Colleville

Arromanches

Courseulles

Lion-sur-Mer

mbieres

Blay

BAYEUX

Cnd 3 Inf

Doines

Oustreham

Merville

6 A B

711 Inf

7 Arm

716 Inf (−)

Lehr Pzr

12 SS Pzr

3 Inf

ebisey

Inf

346 Inf

Bures

d

Berigny

Tilly-sur-Seulles

Carpiquet

21 Pzr

CAEN

XXX

LXXXVI

XXX
I SS Pzr

Aure River

Caumont

Tourville

Argences

Dires River

May-sur-Orne

Villers-Bocage

Odon River

Orne River

Laison River

In the western part of the Utah area, the 90th *Inf. Div.* was finally committed through the 82nd around Ste. Mère-Eglise, only to find itself caught up in the bocage.

Against the British 50th, the *Panzer Lehr* took up defenses around Tilly-sur-Seulles. They sent their personnel carriers to the rear and dug their tanks in so that the hulls were protected. They even went so far as to obscure the tracks they made pulling into position so that aerial reconnaisance would have a harder time fixing their locations. The result was a very well prepared defensive position that the British would have to work them out of. On the night of the 10th, *Panzer Lehr* launched its own attack to try to get to the coast but it quickly ran into trouble. In order to make their strength appear greater than it was, they had their track-mounted Flak units lower their guns so that they appeared to be tanks. This ruse worked fairly well on the British infantry which, in the night battle, could only see a long barrel on a tracked vehicle and assumed it was a tank. However, the British tankers weren't fooled and the Flak vehicles took heavy losses and had to fall back. Still, attacks on the 10th, which continued into the 11th, did drive within five kilometers of Bayeux.

More significant was the launching of an attack through 50th Division by the 7th Armoured Division. Since Montgomery had given up on taking Caen by direct assault, he decided to try to encircle it. While he would, ideally, have liked a double envelopment, one wing out of the forces east of the Orne and the second from the west, it was on the western wing that he put his greatest expectations. The men of 7th Armoured were veterans of North Africa. They bore the nickname "Desert Rats" and were anxious to show the Germans their skill once more. Unfortunately, they left their Shermans behind and had converted to the new Cromwell tanks. The Cromwell was a cavalry tank, relatively light and fast moving. Intended for a pursuit role, it was not well suited for the fighting in Normandy. The troops felt they were outgunned by the Panther and Tiger tanks. Still, it was hoped that even with *Panzer Lehr* in the line, they could swing around their western flank and trap them in the drive on Caen. The actual jump-off date was to be June 12.

In the center the Canadians were told to prepare to attack on the 12th. Other than that they went about the business of consolidating their holdings and engaging in limited fire fights.

East of the Orne, the 51st (Highland) Division had moved into place with the goal of replacing the 6th Airborne and making an attack to try to take Caen from the east. However, *Kampfgruppe Luck* attacked along with the *346th Inf. Div.* with the result that the 51st was drawn into the battle piecemeal, instead of being able to set its own tempo by launching its own attack. The Germans gained some ground but took heavy infantry casualties, with one battalion down to 100 men in strength. The German attack was unsuccessful in terms of gaining any major terrain objectives but they were successful in spoiling any planned operations of the 51st Division.

June 11, 1944 D+5

Although they had been alerted to attack on June 12, at 0800 the Canadians were advised that the attack would jump off at 1300 that day. There was the expected confusion in changing plans so radically. However, the attack, spearheaded by tanks, moved off on schedule. The lead elements were the 6th Royal Tank Rgt. and the Queen's Own Rifle Rgt. Initially it looked like an easy operation. They passed the original start point of Bretteville and then the new start point, near Norrey-en-Bessin and were heading toward Le Mesnil-Patry when an artillery barrage opened up with the target being Bretteville, in their rear. Almost simultaneously they realized that they had by-passed a strong German force. At about the same time, the Germans opened

Canadian Royal Engineers mill logs for military construction projects.

Before the offensive, soldiers attend a service aboard HMCS Algonquin. *Note British style ships badge on bulkhead at left and "Canada" flash on some sleeves.*

fire and the Canadians found themselves under fire from front and rear. The tanks pressed on toward Le Mesnil-Patry, leaving the infantry to deal with the German infantry. But as they neared the town, they were taken under fire by Germans from the flank and quickly lost five tanks. Another element found itself under fire—from the 50th (Northumbrian) Division, the westernmost unit of XXX Corps. Caught between enemy fire on their left and friendly fire on their right, the Canadians had to fall back. One whole squadron (company) of tanks was trapped and fought to the last vehicle. Even in withdrawal, their way wasn't easy. The route they had taken to advance was now partially blocked by a friendly minefield which the infantry had put in and also by destruction in the town of Norrey-en-Bessin, due to the German shelling. When it was all over, the 6th Royal Tanks had lost 37 tanks and all of its officers. Almost one-third of the total casualties the regiment sustained in Europe occurred on June 11, 1944 at Le Mesnil-Patry.

To replace these two shattered units, the Régiment de la Chaudière and the Fort Garry Horse, a tank unit, were sent in and they dug in between Bray and Rots. The Régiment de la Chaudière, a French-Canadian unit, got a bad taste of fighting by meeting the "Hitler Jugend" the first time out. The French-Canadians sent a patrol into Rots and got back a few walking wounded. The Germans had simply let them walk into a trap before opening fire.

In an attempt to take Rots, 46 Royal Marine Commando was sent in at night. Although the town was taken, the fighting was extraordinarily bloody. The Canadians took the resistance of the "Hitler Jugend" against them as a personal insult. They also made the mistake of dismissing this fierce resistance as mere "Nazi fanaticism." In fact, it was simply an example of a well-trained unit fighting very hard to accomplish its mission: keep the Allies pinned on the beaches and, if possible, push them back into the sea. Tough fighters they undoubtedly were, but political fanaticism was not one of the factors which motivated them in the battle for Normandy.

Elsewhere in the British sector, the *Panzer Lehr* drive on Bayeux was halted as a result of the action at Le Mesnil-Patry. By chance, the reinforcements the Canadians brought up threatened the boundary between *Panzer Lehr* and the "Hitler Jugend," the *12th SS-Panzer*. A boundary between units is always a weakpoint in an army because of the difficulty in controlling across command lines.

Accordingly, *Panzer Lehr* was ordered to go on the defensive in Tilly-sur-Seulles. Because *Panzer Lehr* had attacked before the full division had arrived, once they pulled back into the defense, the late arriving units merely served to solidify the defense that much more. As a result, the British found themselves against a growing defense.

On the eastern-most side, the 51st (Highland) Division was scheduled to make its "left hook" attack on the 11th but the Germans managed to forestall this by a series of attacks launched by *Kampfgruppe Luck*. By this time the Germans had *21st Panzer*, and *346th, 711th*, and *716th Infantry Divisions* against the combined British 3d Infantry and 6th Airborne Divisions.

The 5th Black Watch kicked off the 51st's attack at 0430 on the 11th and promptly stalled, taking 200 casulaties in the process of trying to take Breville.

In the V Corps sector, the Americans were advancing more steadily toward Caumont, some 33 kilometers inland. As a result, the British felt that they might encounter lighter resistance if they shifted their "right hook" attack on Caen further to the west. The 7th Armoured had been trying to penetrate the German lines around Tilly-sur-Seulles all day with no effect and the shift to the right seemed a sound move.

Other than this advance by V Corps, progress in the American sector was excruciatingly slow. The problem was that while the advance on the Forêt de Cerisy and Caumont was welcomed, after the very slow going through the bocage up to that time, it was far more important that Cherbourg be secured and progress toward that goal was at a crawl. Carentan seemed determined to hold out forever; the 4th Division was inching forward in the north and the 90th not even doing that on the western part of the Utah sector. On the other hand, the Germans had not mounted the concerted counterattacks against the Americans which they had against the British/Canadian landings. This really is not surprising, in retrospect. The Germans had the terrain as their ally against the Americans. If Caen fell, the British armor could move out into the open ground beyond Caen and securing a new line would be most difficult.

June 12, 1944 D + 6

On June 11 the U.S. 1st Inf. Div. began to make contact with elements of the *17th SS-Panzergrenadier Division*. It was of considerable concern to First Army that V Corps not get drawn into any kind of battle which would require taking troops from the drive on Cherbourg. Therefore, they had been directed to proceed cautiously throughout the drive on Caumont and the Forêt de Cerisy. The concern was aggravated by the knowledge that the British 7th Arm. Div. just to the east of 1st Inf. Div., was facing *Panzer Lehr* and a large gap was opening up between the British, who were stalled in their drive, and the lead elements of 1st Inf. Div., advancing on Caumont. As a result, 1st Inf. Div. changed its advance to a methodical one, proceeding by phase lines with no one moving beyond a given phase line until all of the forward units had reached it.

American concerns seemed to be justified when the Germans began to threaten the junction between V Corps and VII Corps, at Carentan. The U.S. 2d Arm. Div., which had come ashore and been sent as a reserve behind 1st Inf. Div., was compelled to send a combat command to Carentan as backup against this new threat.

For the British, June 12 was the start date of Montgomery's second major effort to secure Caen. He had been thwarted earlier in trying to take it by direct assault. The "left hook" to be mounted by 51st Highland Division had been stopped by the preemptive attacks of *Kampfgruppe Luck* and the rest of the *21st Pz Div*.

Now 7th Arm. Div. was to try a "right hook" through the town of Villers-Bocage, to try to encircle Caen to the left; Montgomery had available in England the 1st Airborne Division and he felt that they could be dropped southwest of Caen, near Evrecy, on June 13. This was behind German lines and could disrupt their defenses so

General Barkan of 4th Division greeted by grateful local residents. "Ivy Division" insignia is clearly visible on his officer's pattern OD shirt.

82nd Airborne in St. Marie-du-Mont, June 12. MPs
keep a sharp eye on windows.

badly that the "left hook" would succeed. His problem was Air Marshall Sir Trafford Leigh–Mallory, the former head of British Fighter Command and now over-all head of Allied air operations for Overlord. It was Montgomery who first conceived the airborne drops for D-Day; Leigh-Mallory had opposed them. Although events proved Montgomery's assessment valid, Leigh-Mallory still felt the cost outweighed the benefit.

Maj. Gen. Urquhart, commander of the 1st Airborne, wanted to land in daylight to minimize link-up difficulties on the ground. Air Vice Marshall Hollinghurst, who commanded the transport group which would be involved, claimed that the enemy defenses would be too strong and that only a night landing was possible. Leigh-Mallory then took the position that a night flight was unsafe because the transports might be fired on by the Allied naval vessels still delivering fire support. Of course, that same argument could have applied for the original landings and it is obvious that, given sufficient coordination, the risk of firing on friendly aircraft can be minimized. Because 7th Armoured had to move through the U.S. sector to get into a proper attack position, Montgomery had another day to argue his point—rather than 13th, he wanted it now on the 14th. It made no difference: Leigh-Mallory remained adamant.

The 50th Division attempted to make a frontal assault against *Panzer Lehr* but achieved no real progress. The 7th Armoured, however, swung west through V Corps' sector and managed to get around the flank of *Panzer Lehr*. They met little significant opposition because the operations of the American 1st and 2d Infantry had cut the link between *352d Infantry* and *Panzer Lehr* and there were only elements of the *17th SS-Panzergrenadier* to tie the line together. The forward units of 7th Armoured stopped for the night about 10 kilometers from Villers-Bocage and fully expected to sieze it the next day.

In the Utah sector the frustration at the lack of results was beginning to grow. The 90th Division, which should have taken the lion's share of the work from 82d Airborne, was singularly unsuccessful. The 82d was still nowhere near full strength thanks to the number lost in the initial landing and was not equipped for heavy fighting. It was less mobile and had lighter artillery than a regular infantry division. In the north, 4th Infantry made progress toward Cherbourg but it was clear that something would have to be done of a more dramatic nature if they were to get out of the beachhead area before Fall.

Almost as a sidelight, on the night of June

Crossroads south of St. Côme-du-Mont, known to 101st Airborne as "Dead Man's Corner."

12–13, *Flak Rgt. 155,* located in the Pas de Calais, opened fire with the first V-1's. The V-1 was simply a pulse jet with a warhead. The pulse jet gave it its unique sound and led to its nickname of "buzz bomb." The V-1 was simply aimed in the desired direction and when the engine cut off, it dropped to the ground. The weapon was sub-sonic and the British ultimately found that by diving on it from above, they could get the necessary speed to shoot it down. This first day only four of the ten which were launched actually hit anything in England. However, by the 15th they were able to get off 244 in a 24 hour period. The majority of them struck London and, in the first three weeks, killed 2,752. What is surprising is that none were ever directed against known troop concentrations—or even the feared troop concentrations of the non-existant "First U.S. Army Group." Instead, they were simply used as terror weapons. While it is unlikely that they could have made any difference even if they were directed against such concentrations, at a critical time such as this, anything to delay Allied reinforcement should have been attempted.

U.S. M3 halftrack greeted by French civilians.

June 13, 1944 D +8

The 7th Armoured kicked off its attack on the 13th and by early morning tanks from 4th County of London Yeomanry and half-track-mounted infantry of 1st Battalion the Rifle Brigade were in Villers-Bocage without any apparent opposition. On the other hand, the 8th and 11th Hussars were encountering resistance and were slower in their advance. Moving through the town, they sent a squadron (company) of tanks and another of infantry to sieze Hill 213, which was astride a major road leading directly to Caen.

As they pulled up toward Hill 213, one German observed that they were acting as though they had won the war already. That observer was Hauptsturmführer Michel Witmann, who was a company commander in the *501st SS Heavy Tank Battalion*, part of the corps troops of *I SS-Panzer Corps*. The corps was moving up to add its weight to the operation and Witmann had brought his company from Beauvais, starting June 7, and, travelling by night, had finally arrived in the vincinity of that hill the previous day. Witmann, who had 119 tank kills to his credit while serving with *1st SS-Panzer Division "Leibstandarte Adolf Hitler"* in Russia, had expected to spend the 13th in maintenance on his company's Tiger tanks after the long move up. Instead, he was confronted by the lead elements of 7th Armoured and decided to take matters into his own hands. What followed was probably the most dramatic single tank operation of the war. He opened fire and immediately one of the British half-tracks went up in flames. He then proceeded down the line, destroying half-track after half-track. The lead Cromwell he encountered fired first. The 6-pounder round just bounced off the Tiger's armor and the Cromwell quickly became a ball of flame. Proceeding into the town, he came upon four tanks of the headquarters group of the London Yeomanry, three of which were promptly destroyed, the fourth only avoiding a similar fate because the driver backed out of danger. One tank of B Squadron managed to get a flank shot and fired three rounds at Witmann's Tiger before the hand-traversed turret of the Tiger could swing around. One of the rounds actually produced some smoke and there was some hope they might have caused some damage. Witmann's reaction was to send a round into the building next to the British tank, bringing down a hail of bricks which buried the tank. In about five minutes of fighting, Witmann had knocked out 25 armored vehicles.

Witmann then withdrew, refueled and re-supplied and returned to the vicinity of Hill 213 with four other Tigers, destroying what remained of the British force there. Later in the day, he returned to the village itself with elements of *2d Pz Div.*, now moving into the area. The British were ready this time and Witmann's tank, as well as three other Tigers were knocked out, but the German crews all escaped because there were no British infantry left to take them prisoner. Still later in the day, a mixed batch of troops from *Panzer Lehr* as well as infantry from *2d Panzer* moved into the town and the British were finally forced to break off and withdraw to Tracy-Bocage, some three km to the west. The day's operations had cost the British 25 tanks, 14 half-tracks and 14 Bren carriers. Effectively, the spearhead of 7th Armoured had been destroyed. As an epilog, Witmann survived the battle and on June 22, in apparent recognition of this engagement, he was awarded the swords to the Knight's Cross, the second highest of the regular German awards. However, on August 8, 1944, he was reported missing in action, apparently killed with his crew in one of the massive bombing raids the Allies used to break out of the bocage.

In the V Corps area, having taken Caumont, the attack ground to a halt. The *17th SS-Panzergrenadier* element encountered was actually the division reconnaissance battalion. The rest of the division had been inserted near Carentan and was attacking there against the juncture between the two U.S. corps. However, while the Americans were being cautious, the Germans were reinforcing. The *2d Panzer* was in action on the 13th and the *3d Fallschirmjager Division* was in place by that time too. As a result, the gap which only the *17th SS*'s reconnaissance battalion was holding, was now solidified with two capable units.

In the Utah area, dissatisfied with the lack of progress on the part of the 90th Division, Collins, the corps commander, sacked two regimental commanders and the division commander, replacing the latter with his own assistant corps commander Maj. Gen. Landrum. Collins pulled the 90th out of the line and put the 9th Inf. Div. under Maj. Gen. Eddy, in its place. He also asked that the 79th Inf. Div. be assigned to the corps in case the change-over in the 90th was not successful. Collins gave the 82d and 9th the mission of driving west and cutting the Cotentin Peninsula, preventing the Germans from putting more reinforcements into the defense of Cherbourg.

Browning .30 caliber medium machine gun, here used by 82nd Airborne troopers fighting as regular infantry.

June 14, 1944 D + 8

The joint attack by the 82d and 9th made good progress. Because each had a regiment off on other duties, they could only use two regiments for the operation but each proceeded with both available regiments up on line. By rotating the lead battalion two or three times a day, they were able to set up a steady pace westward.

Montgomery decided to go on the defensive everywhere but around Caumont. However, the *2d Panzer Div.*, whose move from the Abbeville area had gone undetected, put a serious crimp in British plans.

The 7th Armored soon found themselves attacked from three sides. The *2d Pz Div.* launched an attack in the vicinity of Caumont and by dark had forced the British off Hill 174, near Cahagnes, and had almost cut the Caumont-Amaye-sur-Orne road. Only by calling on the adjacent American corps for artillery support were they able to break the attack of *2d Panzer*. It was obvious that the 7th Armored was in an untenable position. Accordingly, after dark, they pulled back to the vicinity of Caumont. It would be another six weeks before they returned to Villers-Bocage.

At the same time, the 50th Division launched an attack in their area but made relatively limited gains. They were, by this time, worn down and tired and the *Panzer Lehr*, against which they were fighting, was determined not to let the British advance. The British were simply stalemated in front of Caen.

For all Mongomery's later protestations that he ws proceeding according to plan, the British forces faced the very realistic possibility that the Germans had made their lines strong enough to stop the British in their tracks. Between the two allies, the British had a much more bitter experience in the static warfare of World War I and, having been fighting since 1939, were not up to the manpower cost of fighting a static warfare battle. They, more than the Americans, needed a war of mobility simply because they had about reached the end of their manpower pool and could not afford heavy losses.

CHAPTER IV

SECURING A PORT
June 15, 1944 D+9

Montgomery called off efforts to take Caen for a period of two days. Things were beginning to go quite well for the Americans in their drive westward out of the Utah area. 325th Glider Rgt of 82d Airborne Division was within a kilometer of St. Sauveur-le-Vicomte, through which passed the only good north-south road in the center of the peninsula. It would have a major effect on the ability of the Germans to reinforce for any defense of Cherbourg. Elsewhere in the Utah area, there was little progress.

The fighting in the British sector had been intense as the Germans sought to stabilize their lines and the British tried to find a hole they could get through. The Germans lacked the force to push the British back into the sea but they did have the force necessary to contain them. Therefore, they contented themselves with local attacks, all attempting to improve their position but none undertaken with any expectation of major gains. The British, for their part, were busy assessing how to crack the German positions because nothing they had tried to that point was successful.

Because of the cover plan that the Normandy landings were to be portrayed as merely the first of at least two and perhaps three, the Allies had not bombed the Loire Bridges. Bombing those bridges would have had no effect on operations in the Pas de Calais but it would have the effect of sealing off the approaches to Normandy from south of the Loire, where a considerable number of German divisions sat idly by. On June 15 the Allies decided to abandon one part of the pretense and launched a bombing raid on the Loire bridges, knocking out eight completely and damaging all of them. Since the Seine River bridges had previously been attacked (that operation would also have been consistent with an effort to prevent reinforcement of the Pas de Calais region by troops from

further west) this new bombing effectively sealed off Normandy and Brittany from major reinforcements. The Germans would have to fight with what they had on hand.

June 16, 1944   D+10

Because 9th Inf. Div. had been held up by German counterattacks, the plan for VII Corps was to have 82d Airborne spearhead the attack with the 9th echeloned to the right, tying in with 79th Inf. Div. on the north side of the VII Corps area. However, before noon of the 16th, 325th Glider Infantry Rgt was on the right bank of the Douve, opposite St. Sauveur. Maj. Gen. Ridgeway, commander of the 82d, requested permission from Collins to cross immediately. Permission was granted and the 505th and 508th Parachute Rgts were directed to secure a bridgehead on the west bank of the Douve.

Anticipating that the German *91st Inf. Div.* might be collapsing, Collins changed his directive to 9th Infantry Division and ordered that they attack directly west and try to come abreast of 82d Airborne, securing their own bridgehead over the Douve. By nightfall, part of 2d Battalion, 60th Inf. Rgt, part of the 9th, was across the Douve along with the elements of the 82d. The Douve River was the last major water obstacle before the coast.

The situation in the British sector seemed so secure that King George VI was brought into France, to speak with the troops at Mongomery's headquarters at Creuilly.

June 17, 1944   D+11

The *2d Pzr Div,* after a break in the fighting, resumed its attacks against the 7th Armoured,

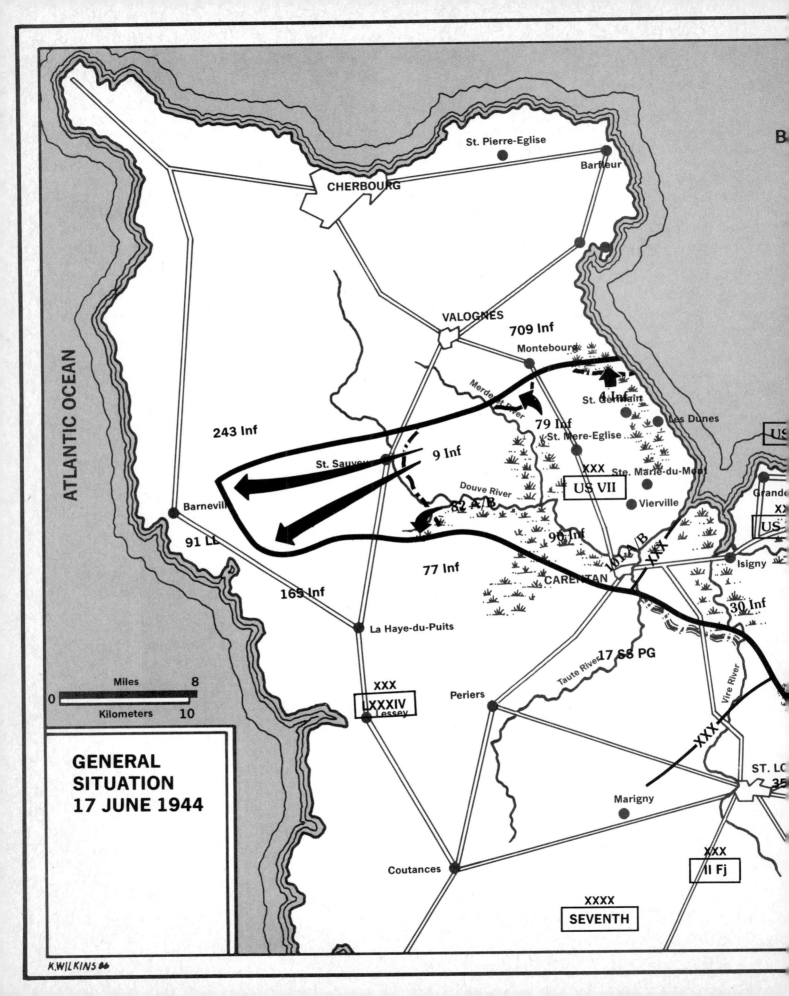

St. Pierre-Eglise

Barfleur

CHERBOURG

VALOGNES

709 Inf

Montebourg

Merderet River

4 Inf

St. Germain

Les Dunes

243 Inf

79 Inf

St. Mere-Eglise

9 Inf

St. Sauveur

Douve River

XXX

Ste. Marie-du-Mont

US VII

Vierville

Barneville

82 A/B

90 Inf

101 A/B

XXX

Grand

US

91 LE

Isigny

US

165 Inf

77 Inf

CARENTAN

30 Inf

La Haye-du-Puits

17 SS PG

Taute River

Vire River

XXX

XXX

LXXXIV

Lessey

Periers

Marigny

ST. LO

35

**GENERAL
SITUATION
17 JUNE 1944**

Miles   8

0

Kilometers   10

Coutances

XXX

II Fj

XXXX

SEVENTH

ATLANTIC OCEAN

K.WILKINS 86

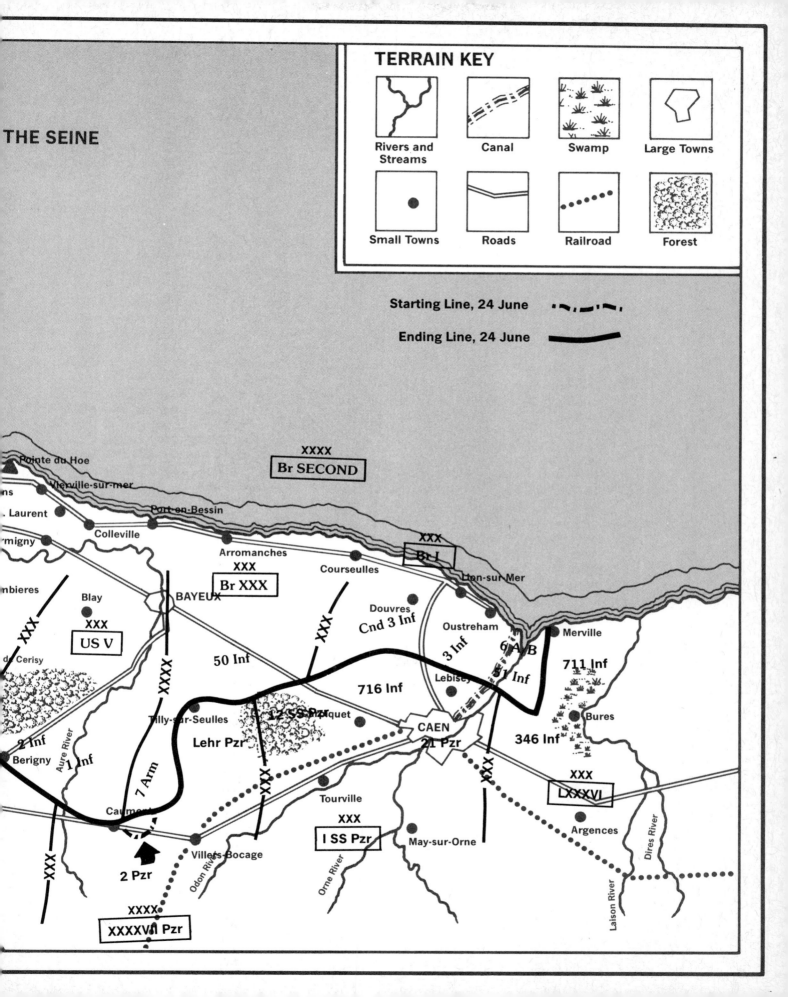

THE SEINE

TERRAIN KEY

Rivers and Streams	Canal	Swamp	Large Towns
Small Towns	Roads	Railroad	Forest

Starting Line, 24 June

Ending Line, 24 June

XXXX
Br SECOND

Pointe du Hoe

Vierville-sur-mer

Port-en-Bessin

. Laurent

Colleville

Arromanches

Courseulles

XXX
Br I

Lion-sur-Mer

migny

XXX
Br XXX

BAYEUX

Douvres

Oustreham

Merville

mbieres

Blay

XXX
US V

Cnd 3 Inf

3 Inf

6 A/B

711 Inf

d/ Cerisy

50 Inf

716 Inf

Lebisey

51 Inf

Bures

Tilly-sur-Seulles

12 SS Pzr

quet

CAEN

346 Inf

2 Inf

Lehr Pzr

21 Pzr

1 Inf

Berigny

Aure River

7 Arm

Tourville

XXX
LXXXVI

Caumont

XXX
I SS Pzr

May-sur-Orne

Argences

Dires River

Villers-Bocage

Odon River

Orne River

Laison River

2 Pzr

XXXX
XXXXVII Pzr

using its left hand elements. These were the units which had been forced to break off their initial attacks due to U.S. artillery fire support for 7th Armoured on June 13. They formed a kampfgruppe out of infantry from the *304th Panzergrenadier Rgt* and tanks from the tank regiment. The objective was Le Quesnay. The attack jumped off at 0430 and quickly reached the outskirts of the town where they encountered a sunken road bordered by hedges. The bocage of France favored the defender, regardless of who was cast in that role. This time it was the British who got the advantage of it. The British were ready with tanks and infantry and the fighting soon attracted the attention of RAF Typhoons in the air over the battle, which joined in the fighting. The lack of a credible presence in the air by the Luftwaffe made Allied operations against German tanks especially devastating because unless German Flak knocked them out, the Allied planes had a field day.

The fighting was furious as the Germans first secured most of the town and then, behind a rolling barrage of artillery, the British reentered the town to take it back again. The net result was that the original front line was restored, at heavy cost on both sides.

The rapid build-up on the shore caused Montgomery to alter the date for renewing the offensive against Caen to June 22 in light of the expected arrival of the necessary follow-on forces.

In the meantime, 82d and 9th Divisions charged forward against collapsing resistance from the German *91st Division*. Collins was taking a risk in sending these divisions forward without concern for his flanks. However, it was his belief that the Germans had nothing available to throw into the area which could threaten his flanks or else they would have done so long before, when it looked as though the Americans were getting momentum on the drive west and before they reached St. Sauveur.

Hitler arrived in France for a conference to be held at a headquarters known as W II. W II was located in Margival, not far to the northeast of Soissons. Although it had been constructed in 1940 as the command post for the invasion of Britain, in fact it was first used for this conference. Notice of the conference was given only on the evening of June 16, barely giving Rommel enough time to get there since he had been involved in a tour of the front.

Rommel gave his appraisal of the situation and, despite Hitler's insistance that Cherbourg be held, predicted its fall with surprising accuracy as to the date.

Hitler had earlier declared that, in addition to Cherbourg, Ijmuiden, Walcheren Island, Dunkirk, Calais, Cap Gris Nez, Boulogne, Dieppe, Le Havre, St. Malo, Brest, Lorient, St. Nazaire, La Pallice, Royan, and the mouth of the Gironde were to be treated as fortresses. None of these were truly built up to be fortresses, but

U.S. supply depot near beaches July 8th. Soft ground has been reinforced with metal plates.

they did tie up some 200,000 men. Rommel was insistant that Hitler abandon this course of action and free these troops and their equipment for fighting. Hitler was insistant. In fact, except for several which the Allies thought they needed, such as Cherbourg and Brest, most of the ports were allowed to sit quietly in the backwater of the war, with a minimal force left to keep an eye on them. They surrendered in May, 1945, along with the general surrender, having added nothing positive to the defense of Germany.

Rommel had concluded that there would be no second landing further east and requested freedom of action in the area, as well as the assignment of Panzer divisions and adequate air cover. He anticipated that the Allies would try to break out around Caen and also around the Cotentin Peninsula, heading south and then toward Paris with a secondary operation west into Brittany.

Rommel needed the authority to deal with the breakthrough to the sea by the First Army on the west coast of the Cotentin Peninsula as well as authority to withdraw the Caen front behind the Orne River, believing that Caen was not that valuable to hold but was a means for the Allies to bleed off scarce German strength. Von Rundstedt supported Rommel in this position.

Hitler then went into a discussion of the benefits of the V-1 in bringing England to its knees, at which Rommel requested they be directed against the Allied forces on the beach. However, GdArt. Heinemann, the general in charge of the V-1's, indicated that the margin of error in the V-1 was on the order of twelve to twenty kilometers and therefore an attempt to hit the Allied soldiers might just as well hit friendly troops. Hitler turned down the request.

Rommel pointed out that Hitler was attempting to refute all of his arguments by using opinions presented by people who had never been to the front. Apparently the remark stung Hitler because after Rommel and von Rundstedt left, a call was made to line up a visit by Hitler to the front. However, without warning the visit was called off and Hitler went back to Germany. Shortly after Rommel and von Rundstedt left, a V-1 had landed near the headquarters, doing little damage but convincing Hitler someone was trying to kill him.

The main German problem was that they

Breakfast at Jurvigny.
4th Division anti-tank
gunners, August 11.

didn't have enough strength for more than limited counterattacks. However, they hoped to remedy this with the arrival of *II SS-Panzer Corps* in the area, giving them three Panzer corps directed against the British facing Caen: *I SS, II SS,* and *XXXXVII. II SS-Panzer Corps* consisted of two more Panzer divisions—*9th* "Hohenstaufen" and *10th SS-Panzer Division* "Frundsberg". all under the command of the reconstituted *Panzergruppe West*. Their attack against the British to cut them off from the sea was never launched because the heavy Allied shelling prevented bringing up infantry divisions to relieve them of their place in the line.

American truck comes ashore July 21st. Round plate on bumper indicates size of bridge vehicle can cross safely.

Wreckage of Mulberry after June 19th storm.

June 18, 1944 D + 12

At 0500 on June 18 9th Inf. Div. cut the west coast road at Barneville. The Cotentin Peninsula was now cut in two. The question now was what to do about driving on Cherbourg. How strong the defenses of this "fortress" really were was problematical but it was obvious that the faster the Americans moved, the more likely they were to beat the Germans to the punch and get there before the Germans were able to organize the Cherbourg defenses.

Bradley had VIII Corps, under Maj. Gen. Tory Middleton, ready to go and he promptly made them operational to free units to head north while still being ready to hold off any German efforts to reopen the peninsula. VIII Corps took over 82d Airborne and 90th Infantry Divisions, while VII had the 4th, 79th and 9th Divisions to drive on Cherbourg. The attack was to begin at 0400 the next morning. That meant that 9th Infantry Division had to resupply and turn 90° in a relatively short period of time. But, because of the level to which they had been trained, they were able to do just that.

June 19, 1944 D + 13

June 19 will best be remembered as the day of the Storm. The two Mulberries had been operational for just a few days when a storm blew up the channel and destroyed the American Mulberry. The scope of the destruction tended to make it seem as if there had been a much stronger wind than in fact accompanied the storm. Lulled by the reference to the Mulberry as an artificial harbor, some took the view that the supply ships were better off inside the Mulberry than out at sea. Of course, the Mulberry was no such thing. At best it was a series of piers and it was an artificial harbor in the sense that materiel could be landed there when previously there had been no such facilities. But it lacked the natural protection which goes with natural harbors. Many of the captains of the supply ships, recognizing that their vessels had been built to take the pounding of the mid-Atlantic, at its worst, pulled out into the North Sea. When the storm blew itself out, many of the ships which had sought shelter inside the Mulberry were driven on to the beaches. The

American Mulberry was utterly destroyed and the British one seriously damaged. Fortunately, there was enough left of the American Mulberry to fix the British one so the Allies were not totally deprived of a means to off-load the supply ships. But many came to believe that the Mulberry was not merely a make-shift operation but, in fact, the sole means by which they could be supplied. The loss of one and damage to the other caused serious concern among some Allied leaders. They needed a real port.

The Allies, thanks to the work of British cryptographers, had managed to read the signals of the German high command. While this did not always yield critical information, at this juncture it did. Collins learned that the Germans had split their *77th Inf Div* in two, part to shield Cherbourg and part to maintain communications with the rest of the German armed forces in France. Further, he learned that permission had been granted to GL von Schlieben, now commander of both Cherbourg and the *709th Inf Div* to withdraw his forces into the Cherbourg fortifications. Collins felt, rightly, that the best time to attack an enemy was as they were trying to retreat.

However, the same weather which destroyed the Mulberry hindered Collins' advance. Great gains were made on the first day, especially in the 9th Inf. Div. sector, but they were initially slower in the sectors of 79th and 4th Divisions. Still, it was apparent that there would be no fighting outside of Cherbourg.

June 20, 1944 D + 14

Collins' attack continued moving right up the width of the Cotentin Peninsula, with the right flank of the attack now catching up with 9th Inf. Div. The previous day's storm continuing into the 20th, hindered the American advance or they might well have drawn up against the Cherbourg defenses on the 20th.

In the British area the on-going storm threw their planned resumption of the attack on Caen completely off time-table. Three additional divisions planned to be landed for the operation were all sitting in England waiting for the storm to die down.

Mail call for American troops, June 21, 1944. 1st Infantry Division patch can be easily distinguished despite censor's efforts.

Normandy farms made a contribution to the Allied war effort. The limited visibility and field of fire in the background was typical of the bocage country.

June 21, 1944 D+15

As "the worst June storm in the Channel in forty years" blew itself out, US VII Corps continued its advance on Cherbourg. Collins tried to instill a special sense of urgency in the troops so that they would take Cherbourg rapidly in light of the loss of Mulberry-A in the American zone.

June 22, 1944 D+16

During the night of June 21–22, Collins sent an ultimatum to GL von Schlieben, the German commander in the "fortress" of Cherbourg, fixing 0900 of the 22d as the deadline for him to surrender his troops. Collins now had three divisions poised against von Schlieben's forces. The deadline, however, passed without response. Anticipating this, Collins had set 1400 as the time for the assault to begin. Prior to this, there would be an aerial bombardment of Cherbourg.

This aerial operation was the biggest since D-Day and involved 557 fighter-bombers, and 396 bombers, all out of the Ninth Air Force, and 118 additional planes from the Second Tactical Air Force. The artillery of VII Corps marked the boundaries of the German defenses with white smoke. First in were six squadrons of Mustangs and four of Hawker Typhoons, the former strafing everything in sight and the latter attacking with rockets. These were followed by twelve groups of fighter-bombers which bombed and strafed until five minutes before H-Hour. They then shifted to eleven strongpoints while the soldiers began their attack on the three ridges surrounding Cherbourg.

Collins was surprised that the Germans didn't hold on to the outer ridges but, instead, retreated to the inner fortifications. The troops defending Cherbourg were parts of divisions which were not all that battle-worthy to begin with and had been worn down by previous fighting.

The battle for Cherbourg quickly became a battle for pillboxes and bunkers. The Americans

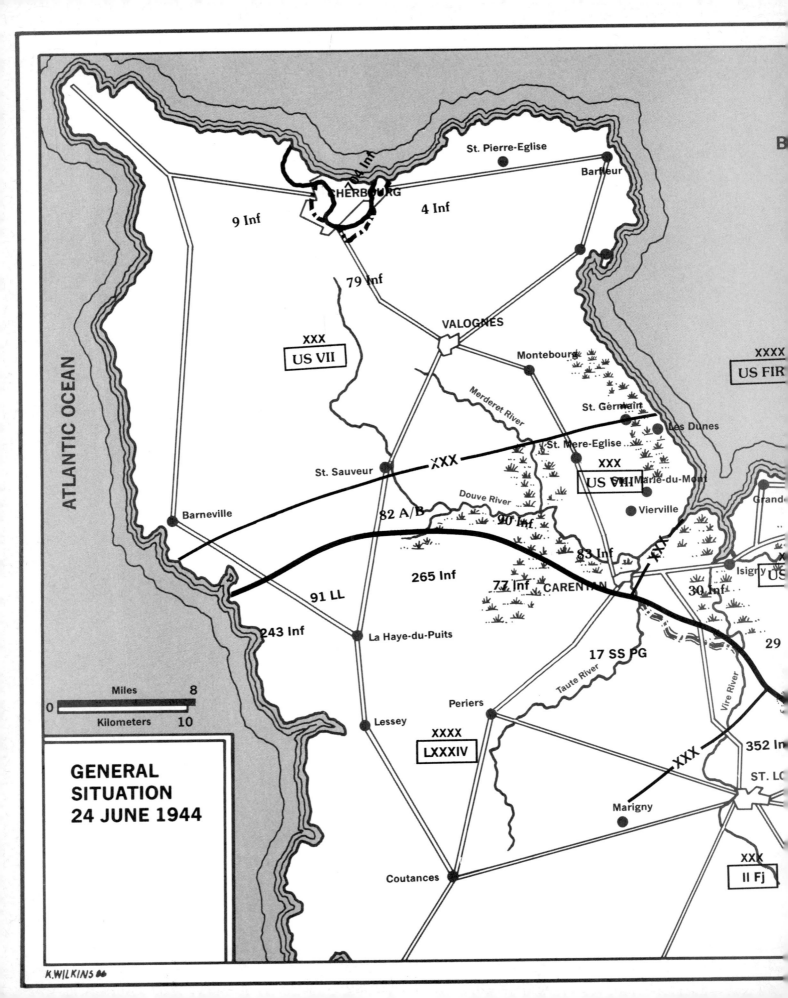

ATLANTIC OCEAN

St. Pierre-Eglise

Barfleur

04 Inf

CHERBOURG

9 Inf

4 Inf

79 Inf

VALOGNES

Montebourg

XXX
US VII

Merderet River

St. Germain

Les Dunes

St. Mere-Eglise

XXX
US VIII

Marie-du-Mont

St. Sauveur

XXX

Barneville

Douve River

Vierville

82 A/B

90 Inf

Grand

XXXX
US FIR

265 Inf

83 Inf

Isigny

US

XXX

91 LL

77 Inf

CARENTAN

30 Inf

243 Inf

La Haye-du-Puits

29

Miles   8

17 SS PG

0

Kilometers   10

Taute River

Vire River

Lessey

Periers

GENERAL
SITUATION
24 JUNE 1944

XXXX
LXXXIV

XXX

352 In

ST. LO

Marigny

XXX
II Fj

Coutances

K.WILKINS 86

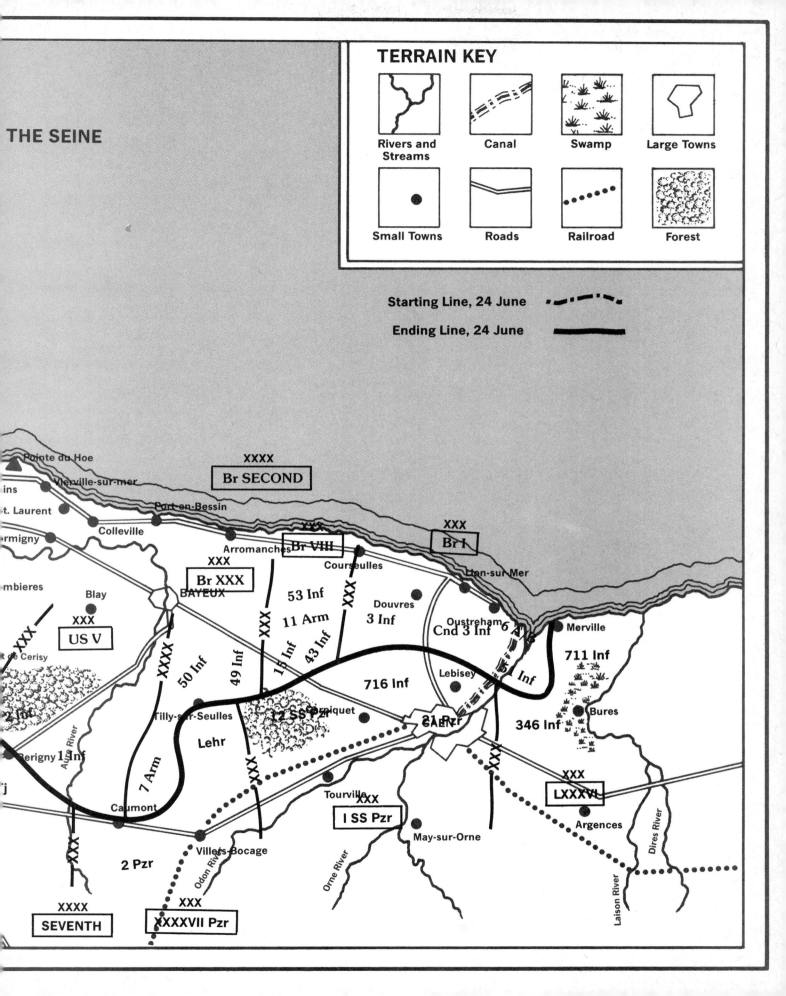

THE SEINE

TERRAIN KEY

Rivers and Streams	Canal	Swamp	Large Towns
Small Towns	Roads	Railroad	Forest

Starting Line, 24 June

Ending Line, 24 June

Pointe du Hoe

Vierville-sur-mer

ins

St. Laurent

Port-en-Bessin

XXXX
Br SECOND

Colleville

rmigny

Arromanches

XXX
Br VIII

Courseulles

XXX
Br I

Lion-sur-Mer

XXX
Br XXX

BAYEUX

mbieres

Blay

XXX
US V

53 Inf

11 Arm

Douvres

3 Inf

Oustreham 6 A

Cnd 3 Inf

Merville

t de Cerisy

XXXX

50 Inf

49 Inf

15 Inf

43 Inf

716 Inf

Lebisey

5 Inf

711 Inf

346 Inf

Bures

2 Inf

Aure River

Tilly-sur-Seulles

12 SS Pzr

rniquet

21 Pzr

Berigny 1 Inf

Lehr

7 Arm

XXX

Tourville

XXX
LXXXVI

Argences

Dires River

j

Caumont

XXX
I SS Pzr

May-sur-Orne

Villers-Bocage

2 Pzr

Odon River

Orne River

Laison River

XXXX
SEVENTH

XXX
XXXXVII Pzr

developed an effective technique for dealing with these fixed positions. They would creep within 300 meters under artillery cover, have machineguns and anti-tank weapons fire into the slits of the bunker in order to keep the defender from firing on the attackers, then send demolition teams in which would blow the rear doors with charges, followed by phosphorus grenades and other types of explosives thrown inside to eliminate the defenders.

Hitler called upon his troops to defend Cherbourg to the last bunker and to turn the town into a field of ruins. Hitler also tried to appeal to their patriotism by noting that the honor of the Germany Army depended on how well they fought. As the defenders were not only German but also French, Russian, and Polish, it is doubtful that the honor of the Germany Army meant much to them.

In their sector, the British were working hard to start another attack on Caen. Previous efforts had been single-division attacks—the Canadian 3d Division initially, the 50th and 51st from separate directions, later, and the 7th Armoured at Villers-Bocage. All had failed and the Germans had built up their own forces to the point that a single-division attack was now out of the question.

Accordingly, this new operation, code-named Epsom, would be launched by five fresh divisions, the 49th (West Riding) Division, to be assigned to XXX Corps, and four divisions in a new VIII Corps, to be inserted between XXX and I Corps. VIII Corps would consist of 15th (Scottish), 43d (Wessex), 53d (Welsh), and 11th Armoured Division. The corps was commanded by Lt. Gen. Sir Richard O'Connor, who had distinguished himself in North Africa during the first British campaign, only to be captured later in 1941. Freed on the fall of Italy, O'Connor was given three of the finest divisions the British had available. The attack was to begin June 25 and the initial objective was the Odon River, southwest of Caen.

June 23, 1944 D+17

The advance into Cherbourg went slowly, but by the 23d, the Americans detected a weakening of resistance. Moreover, they were starting to work their way through the thickest defensive belt into the more open areas behind, reaching the stage where they were able to attach tanks to the forward companies and pick up the pace of their advance.

Because the effort was to break the German resistance, rather than simply ferret out every possible pocket, the Americans by-passed areas where they weren't fired upon, with some curious results. Among the places which were by-passed was the German central switchboard, with the result that GL von Schlieben could get a detailed, current situation right to the end. Not, of course, that he could do much about what he heard. It is doubtful that he ever entertained any serious notion that he could hold out long enough to get relieved by some German counterattack. All he saw was that he had a mission of fighting the Americans as hard as he could and holding them off from gaining the port as long as he could, with an additional goal of doing what he could to ensure that the port they did capture was rendered as useless as possible due to the fighting.

June 24, 1944   D+18

On June 24, the divisions of the VII Corps began to enter the city itself. This added the element of street fighting to the problem of bunkers and pillboxes. Von Schlieben tried to stimulate resistance by liberally handing out iron crosses but it was a losing cause by that time for all but the most optimistic.

28th Division routs sniper, August 2.

CHAPTER V

EPSOM
June 25, 1944 D+19

The British plan for Epsom was relatively simple. The 49th West Riding Division, on the eastern flank of XXX Corps, would attack on the 25th to secure high ground around Fontenay and Rauray. The following day, the VIII Corps would attack, led by 15th Scottish, aided by the 31st Tank Brigade and the 4th Armoured Brigade. Behind the 15th would come the 43rd Wessex to mop up anything left behind by the advance, and the 11th Armoured, which was prepared to break out and execute the left hook around Caen once the infantry had secured the crossings over the Odon. At the same time, the Canadians were expected to advance and take Carpiquet Airfield, outside of Caen, while the 51st Highland Division would swing out of the easternmost part of the British positions to try to envelope Caen in a pincer.

At 0415, behind a creeping barrage which advanced toward the enemy, the attack began. However, nature played a trick not long after the advance started, which threw the whole operation off. Ground fog hung in the low spots which seemed to swallow the advancing infantry. Control quickly broke down as no one knew where anyone else was. As the advancing soldiers finally encountered the Germans, the fog made it impossible for the defenders to make use of their long-range weapons—they couldn't see anything to shoot. Instead, the morning deteriorated into bitter hand-to-hand fighting.

By noon they had a foothold on the edge of Fontenay, but there the advance bogged down. The Germans sent in tanks, including Tigers, and although the British fought them off and were even able to bring up a few Shermans to give them their own tank force, they were forced to dig in for the night around Fontenay. Critically, they had failed to take Rauray. The high ground around Rauray gave the Germans

heights from which to fire on the 15th Scottish the following day.

Sepp Dietrich, Hitler's old crony and commander of *I SS-Panzer Corps* ordered the heavy tank company, which was located in the path of the anticipated advance of VIII Corps, to counterattack the next morning. This was over the strong objection of the *12th SS-Panzer*, which saw this heavy tank company as a key factor in the expected attack. From Dietrich's point of view, a breakthrough had occurred which threatened to separate *12th SS-Panzer* from *Panzer Lehr*.

On the west, Collins decided to ask for help from naval gunnery in his assault on Cherbourg. They were able to bring up three American battleships—*Arkansas, Texas* and *Nevada*—as well as four cruisers and a complement of destroyers. Spotting was provided by Spitfires, some of them flown by Americans because of their familiarity with American gunnery procedures. In general, their efforts against the Cherbourg gun emplacements were ineffective. The whole purpose of these emplacements was to withstand naval gunnery and their true weak spots were against high angle fire or bombs. The direct fire of the navy guns simply took on the defense at its strongest.

The naval fire was valuable against less substantial emplacements, such as 88s which the Germans had put in unprepared positions and the impact of the naval gunnery had a demoralizing effect on the Germans. From the American point of view, the left and right flank defenses of Cherbourg had collapsed by the end of the 25th and only in the center was there much resistance.

June 26, 1944   D + 20

At 0730 the 15th Scottish Division began its advance on Caen. In front of the Scots was a German defensive belt established through a series of individual positions which had interlocking fields of fires on each side. This initial position was not intended to be held at all costs. Its primary purpose was to slow the enemy advance and cause them to deploy prematurely. Once that was done, the defenders were expected to pull out and fall back to where a much stronger defense would be offered. The Germans had been working on these for a number of weeks, ever since the effort of the 50th and Canadian Third Divisions to make a direct attack on Caen had failed. As a result, the Germans were well dug in. Behind this first line was what the Germans called the Advance Position, a second defensive belt, located about 6 km from the start line of the attack. This was a much stronger position, using minefields and lying within range of medium artillery. Another five km behind that was the Main Position. Actually, it was hoped that the Main Position would not have to be used. Ideally, the attacker would be stopped at the Advance Position. This defensive technique was relatively new to the German Army, having been developed in Russia, where the Germans were having to fight more and more defensive battles and had become good at it.

The barrage to kick off the 15th Scottish Division's attack drew on both land-based artillery and naval gunnery, but the Germans were veterans and not the poor quality soldiers being encountered around Cherbourg. As soon as the Scots advanced, they came under fire. The day was rainy and by the time the Scots got to Cheux, they were starting to experience control problems, with elements getting lost in the orchards around the town. They were also experiencing difficulty in coordinating their tank activities, since Cheux had been pounded to rubble and the Churchill tanks were primarily valuable for their armor, not their mobility. When the Churchills did open fire with their machineguns, the tracers flew all around, causing consternation to both German and British troops. The Germans were especially adept at homing in on tanks which carelessly exposed themselves, creating more caution on the part of the tanks than the situation should have required.

On the western side of what was becoming known as the "Scottish Corridor," the 49th West

Sergeant of 9th Infantry Division outside Marigny, July 28.

Riding was still trying to reach its objectives of the previous day. In fact Fontenay was still not cleared and half of Tessel Wood was still in German hands. The 49th made an effort to attack toward Rauray out of Tessel but without success. Finally, as the day drew on, the feeling among the Germans was that the 49th was being held but the 15th appeared to be a real threat. Accordingly, elements of the *12th SS-Panzer Rgt* were sent to attack the 15th Scottish in its flank.

The attack, mounted by PzKpfw IV's caught the attacking 23d Hussars (of the 11th Arm. Div.) by surprise. When their lead Shermans burst into flames they pulled back behind a hill to resupply and refuel and wait out the night. Meanwhile the German tanks pressed on and halted for the night on the east side of Le Haut du Bosc.

At Cherbourg, a captured German gave the Americans the location of von Schlieben's command post. The Americans went to it, again demanded a surrender and when that wasn't forthcoming, tank destroyers began firing into the tunnel entrances leading to the command post. That was sufficient for von Schlieben, who then personally surrendered. However, he refused to surrender for the entire garrison. Although Maj. Gen. Eddy of the 9th Infantry Division, to whom von Schlieben surrendered, had extended the traditional courtesy of war to von Schlieben by inviting him to his command post for lunch, when Bradley learned that von Schliebean refused to order the entire garrison to surrender, he refused to participate. As it was, aside from von Schlieben, they had captured the German naval commander of Cherbourg and some 800 soldiers.

June 27, 1944 D + 21

With the surrender of GM Sattler, von Schlieben's deputy, with another 400 Germans, organized resistance in Cherbourg ended. At that point, 9th Infantry was sent northwest to clear Cap de la Hague while the 79th was pulled out and sent south to prepare for further operations. The 4th Inf. Div. was given responsibility for reducing the last of the resistance in Cherbourg.On the same day, the 83d Inf. Div. replaced the 101st Airborne in the line. The 101st was sent back to England for rest and refitting.

For the British, the day saw a continuation of the attack. It was planned to have the Scots charge forward and leave follow-on units to worry about the flanks. Spearhead of this new drive was the 2d Argyll & Sutherland Highlanders. They were to take the bridge over the Odon at Tourmauville, some four km to the south.

The Argylls didn't have an easy route to get to the start point because they had to go through Cheux.

The damaged buildings blocked streets and no one took the time to clear them out of the way. As a result, Cheux formed a major bottleneck. The British were limited to whatever could be accomplished by the leading battalions.

British Royal Engineers with armored bulldozers. Rubble-strewn streets were an unexpected impediment to Allied advance.

Artillery

Artillery, especially indirect fire artillery, was responsible for more casualties on the battlefield than any other type of weapon.

Basically, anything above a machinegun in size could be categorized as artillery. There are two basic types—direct fire and indirect fire. Direct fire guns permit the person firing the gun to look at his target and would include anti-tank guns, anti-aircraft artillery, tank guns, assault guns, and certain types of artillery designed to fire directly at the enemy or in an indirect fire mode. Indirect fire involves the gun being elevated to a steeper angle so that whoever fires the gun usually can't see his target. Adjustments of the rounds are furnished by an observer. Though this is now considered the primary artillery role, it has not been around that long since it was impossible in the days before an observer could communicate with the guns. Mortars were the first indirect fire weapons and have been around for several hundred years but they were always set up where the enemy could be seen. With the advent of telephone and wire communications and then radio, the person observing the fall of the round could be a considerable distance away from the guns and artillery fire support changed radically.

In a most technical sense, a gun is a special form of artillery, just like a howitzer. The difference between the two is the ratio between the length of the barrel and the diameter. Roughly speaking, howitzers have barrels which fall between 25 and 35 times the diameter. Longer barrels are generally categorized as guns; shorter are usually mortars.

The artillery of World War II came in a wide variety of forms. The mortar was the most widely available form. On both sides there were small mortars at company level, larger ones at battalion level. At the regimental level, there was usually some sort of heavier artillery, either in the form of a heavy mortar or cannon company. It was the division which had the larger artillery. Mobility was a problem. The majority of artillery in World War II was towed artillery—on both sides. It was slow moving, hard to set up, and couldn't react to changing situations very readily because, once emplaced, it was pretty well fixed as to the direction in which it could fire. Movement to fire in a new direction was not easy. On the other hand, both sides did have self-propelled artillery. The self-propelled artillery involved putting an artillery piece on a tank chassis: For the Germans this was usually the PzKpfw III or IV, though sometimes captured enemy tanks were used, and for the Allies usually the American M3 Grant chassis.

In the area of anti-tank guns, the German and Allied systems were basically quite different. The Germans developed special anti-tank vehicles by taking a tank chassis and adding a more powerful gun and putting considerable armor on the front of the vehicle. German "Jagdpanzers" did not have a turret and therefore had only a limited field of fire. The Allies used the American system. Initially this was an anti-tank gun mounted in an M3 half-track but later it was mounted in its own turret on a Sherman chassis. The anti-tank gun turrets for the U.S. were not heavily armored at all and were often open topped and therefore vulnerable to enemy artillery.

Finally, there was the anti-aircraft artillery. This could be towed or self-propelled and was generally designed, as its name suggests, to give protection against enemy aircraft. However, these guns were often used in other roles and it was through this practice that the Germans found that their 88mm Flak gun was an excellent tank killer. The Germans designated their direct fire guns either as Kampfwagen Kanone (KwK) for tank guns, Flugzeugabwehr Kanone (FlaK) for anti-aircraft and Panzerabwehr Kanone (PaK) for anti-tank tuns. The 88 was the only basic gun to be found in all three configurations.

The smaller weapons were easier to serve because they had a fixed cartridge: the projectile and the powder to fire it were manufactured as a unit. However, the larger pieces tended to have separate bags of powder, which would go in the breech after the projectile.

(continued on next page)

Artillery:

WEAPON	NATION	MAX RANGE (in KM)	TOWED OR SP	COMMENTS
		ANTI-TANK		
37mm M3	US	8	T	
57mm M1	US	10	T	
3″ M5	US	15.4	T/SP	M10 if SP
2 pdr Mk 9	GB	8	T	
6 pdr Mk 2	GB	5.5	T	
17 pdr Mk 1	GB	10	T	
37mm PaK 36	GER	6	T	
50mm PaK 38	GER	3	T	
75mm PaK 40	GER	8.4	T/SP	multiple chassis as SP
88mm PaK 43	GER	14.1	T/SP	Jagdpanther if SP
128mm PaK 44	GER	26.7	T/SP	Jagdtiger if SP
		FIELD ARTILLERY		
75mm How M1	US	9.6	T	
75mm Gun M1897A4	US	13.6	T	
105mm How M2A1	US	12.2	T/SP	m7 Priest if SP
155mm How M1	US	25.4	T/SP	M12 if SP
155mm Gun M1A1	US	25.4	T	"Long Tom"
8″ How M1	US	18.5	T	
8″ Gun M1	US	35.6	T	
240mm How M1	US	25.2	T	
25 pdr M2	GB	13.4	T/SP	Sexton if SP
3.7″ How	GB	6	T	
4.5″ Gun	GB	20	T	
5.5″ Gun	GB	16	T	
7.2″ How Mk6	GB	16.6	T	
75mm leIG 18	GER	4.2	T	
15cm sIG 33	GER	5.1	T/SP	
75mm leFK 18	GER	10.3	T	
105mm leFH 18	GER	11.7	T/SP	
105mm sK 18	GER	20.9	T	
15cm sFH 36	GER	16.5	T	
17cm K 18	GER	32.4	T	
21cm K 39	GER	32.8	T	
24cm K 4	GER	53.6	T	

The Long and Short

			ANTI-AIRCRAFT			
37mm M1A2	US	3.6	T	
40mm M1	US	2.7	T	
3" M3	US	8.5	T	
90mm Gun M2	US	12	T	
105mm M1	US	15.2	T	
120mm M1	US	14.6	T	
40mm Mk1	GB	5	T	
3"	GB	6	T	
3.7" Mk1	GB	9.7	T	
3.7" Mk 6	GB	13.7	T	
4.5"	GB	10.5	T	
5.25" Twin	GB	13.1	T	
20 mm FlaK 38	GER	3.2	SP	quad
30 mm FlaK 38/103	GER	3.5	SP	dual
37 mm FlaK	GER	3.7	SP	
5cm FlaK 41	GER	5.6	T	
88mm FlaK 18,36,37	GER	8	T	
88mm FlaK 41	GER	11.6	T	
105mm FlaK 38	GER	10.6	T	
128mm FlaK 40	GER	11.6	T	

ASSAULT GUNS

75mm StuK 40	GER		SP	Sturmgeschutz III
105mm StuH 42	GER		SP	Sturmgeschutz III

German designations

1e = leicht (light)
s = schwere (heavy)
IG = Infanteriegeschutz (infantry gun)
FH = Feldhaubzite (field howitzer)
FlaK = Fliegerabwehrkanone (aircraft defense cannon)
PaK = Panzerabwehrkanone (armor defense cannon)
StuK = Sturmkanone (assault cannon)

June 28, 1944 D + 22

On the 28th, the Germans made limited counterattacks. They attacked along the railway embankment toward Mouen. The Germans had been shifting available reserves during the previous day. A company from the *21st Pz Div.* was sent to Verson, the headquarters of *12th SS Pz Div.* One of the factors which characterized the performance of the *12th SS-Panzer* was a youthful elan. Many writings have described the division as consisting of teenagers. While this is not quite literally true, in the implicit sense that they were children, they were a young division as a whole. Notions such as "duty" and "honor" had considerable meaning for them and they fought accordingly. The result was that they broke through the defenses at Mouen. Around 1700 the British counterattacked in their turn against the single tank company of the *21st Panzer* which was in the area around Mouen, finally driving them off. In the meantime, the German action kept the 10th Highland Light Infantry pinned in a cornfield there for the better part of the day.

At the head of the drive, in the morning of the 28th, the Argylls were directed to send patrols along the river bank southwest toward Gavrus to see what the status of the bridges were there. They reported back around 1600 that the bridges were intact. At that, the rest of the battalion was directed to follow up and secure the bridgehead at that location.

For the Americans, the 28th was something of a disappointment. The problem was Cherbourg itself. Von Schlieben had assured Hitler that he would not surrender until Cherbourg was rendered useless to the Allies. He was very nearly right. Because they had been able to put the port of Naples back in operation within three days of taking it, the Allies thought they could count on some similar figure for Cherbourg. What they found was that mines were all over the place, all port basins had been blocked by sinking ships in them, all cranes were destroyed, the Gare Maritime, which contained the electrical control system for the port, was destroyed, and 18,000 cubic meters of rubble had been dumped into the basin designed to moor transatlantic steamers. It was expected that a total of 150,000 tons of supplies could be brought in through Cherbourg by July 25. In fact, only 18,000 tons were brought in by that date and it was not until late September that the port was fully operational. By that time, almost every major port on the Channel was in Allied hands. In a very real sense taking Cherbourg had turned out to be a waste of time. Fortunately, the Allies were landing materiel over the beach at an acceptable rate.

June 29, 1944 D + 23

Epsom was clearly not going as planned. By their estimate the British were about 24 hours behind schedule, thanks largely to the traffic jam at Cheux, as well as the inability to push

forward with more than a division at a time. On the 29th, 11th Arm. Div. finally passed through the 15th Scottish and took Hill 112, which dominated the approaches to Caen from the southwest. The Germans were very much aware of the threat this had posed and had already moved to try to deny the British the critical hill, though the units available by then were hardly designed to do the job. The principal defenders at Garvus and Hill 112 were based on a motorized Flak unit, equipped with 88 mm Flak guns, probably the premier anti-aircraft and anti-tank weapon of the war. In a hectic period

of fighting, a number of tanks were lost but so too were a number of the 88's. Late in the afternoon an air strike by Lightnings destroyed a number of guns and finally forced the Flak elements to withdraw to the woods, where the tractors for their guns were located.

What really tipped the balance for the Germans was the arrival of *II-SS Panzer Corps.* This corps had been dispatched, with its two Panzer divisions, *9th* "Hohenstaufen" and *10th* "Frundsberg", shortly after the Allies had landed. Due to Allied air control, it had taken until the 29th for them actually to arrive. An

U.S. soldiers enjoy the benefits of air superiority outside St. Lô, July 25. They illustrate shirtsleeve order with the M1941 windcheater removed common in the summer of 1944.

immediate attack was directed. The *10th* was to attack the Gavrus bridgehead and Hill 112 while the *9th* would attack against le Valtru and Cheux. They were supplemented by two further Waffen-SS divisions. *1st* "Leibstandarte Adolf Hitler" and *2nd* "Das Reich" *SS-Panzer Division*. Both of those divisions were elements of *I SS-Panzer Corps*, which had already been in command of a sector for some time, but, again, the component divisions had been delayed due to Allied air power. "Das Reich" would assist *II SS-Panzer Corps*' attack while "LAH" would assist *12th SS Panzer* in an attack on the eastern flank of the British drive.

The fact that the British were still close to the coast helped because naval gunfire was still available. A near miss from a battleship was enough, for example, to overturn a Panther tank. In addition, Allied air superiority made a significant impact. When the *9th SS-Panzer* was pulling into an assembly area to prepare for an attack toward Cheux, a bomber raid threw all of their preparations off. The result was that the initial attacks were repelled.

However, the feeling was that VIII Corps was exposed and extended too far to withstand such attacks for long. As a result, 11th Ar-

moured was ordered to abandon Hill 112, which was accomplished on the night of June 29–30, as they pulled back to the Odon River line. At the same time, the 53d Division was pushed into the corridor to firm it up. Although the British couldn't go forward, it would be difficult for the Germans to cut them off.

In the western sector, Bradley was planning the next phase of his operation. He was well aware that most of the heavy German reinforcements had gone against Second Army. Still, the advances of V Corps around Caumont had left the Americans with a potentially dangerous situation. Accordingly, Bradley wanted to bring his western corps more on line and planned an operation which would involve VIII Corps starting the attack, followed by VII Corps, which had by this time reoriented from the Cherbourg operation, followed, in turn, by XIX Corps, so that there would be a pivoting movement with V Corps the anchor. The initial objective would be the line Coutances-St. Lo-Caumont. The first attack would begin on July 3, followed by VII Corps on July 4 and XIX Corps on July 7. In the interim, there would be local adjustments on the ground to secure more favorable terrain from which to launch the attack.

Norman peasants mourn fallen Allied soldier. Such spontaneous scenes were common in France and the Low Countries.

CHAPTER VI

SEEKING A BREAKOUT
June 30, 1944 D+24

With the withdrawal of 11th Arm. Div. from Hill 112, Epsom was effectively ended. For the Germans the task was now to try to push back the salient which had been created. As it turned out, the same traffic jam which kept the British from really putting any force forward, now worked to their advantage since there were four divisions in this corridor—15th, 43d, and 53d Infantry and 11th Armoured. German attacks by *II SS-Panzer Corps* were beaten off, as a result, and the war in this area slowly ebbed back to "normal." Not surprisingly, Hitler berated the Waffen-SS divisions for their "unwillingness" to fight. The fact is that fighting in France was far different from Russia. Although the Allies did not have the overwhelming numbers which made Russian successes seem more palatable, they had air superiority and, while they were close to the Channel, naval gun fire. Both of these were not available to the Red Army. As a result, although the Germans nominally outnumbered the British in the Scottish Corridor, the firepower the Allies could bring to bear was devastating. It could—and did—decide battles before the ground troops even closed on each other.

July 1, 1944 D+25

With the coming of July, both sides were eyeing each other cautiously. Although the Germans had apparent superiority in the number of divisions they could bring to bear in the British sector, many of those divisions were seriously reduced in strength. Other than whole divisions coming up to reinforce, the Germans really had no replacements for their losses. Therefore those units which had been fighting hard since the beginning, such as *21st Panzer* and *12th SS-Panzer*, were really shadows of their former selves, making do with pure fighting spirit.

It was apparent to the Germans that Caen could no longer be held. They began to pull out their base units from Caen and evacuate them to the rear. However, there were a few other tricks the Germans had up their sleeves. Frogmen were brought in and briefed on a mission to destroy British-held bridges at Benouville and Ranville, thereby cutting communications across the Orne with the 6th Airborne and 51st Highland Divisions. This would preclude the British from launching any major operations with that easternmost wing of their positions.

While at a conference with Gfm Wilhelm Keitel, head of the OKW and known among the German Army more for his loyalty to Hitler than his military ability, von Rundstedt apparently gave vent to his frustration at the lack of Hitler's military skill and was promptly replaced by a more tractable commander, Gfm Hans Günther von Kluge.

On the other side of the line, the Canadian 3d Division was planning to launch Operation Windsor to capture the airfield and village of Carpiquet, just west of Caen. That operation was set to go on July 4.

July 2, 1944 D+26

In the western sector, VII Corps took over a sector between VIII and XIX Corps, opposite Carentan in preparation for the effort to break clear of the bocage. The British were making their own preparations and on the German side, it was a matter of rest, resupply and wait.

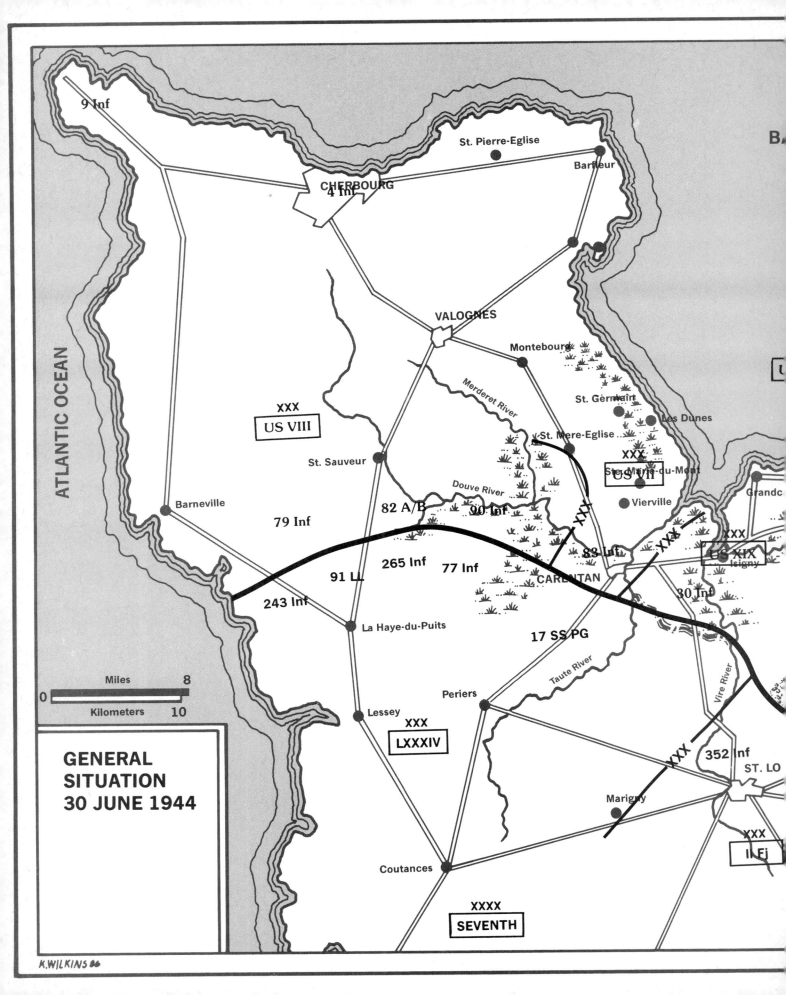

ATLANTIC OCEAN

9 Inf

St. Pierre-Eglise

Barfleur

CHERBOURG
4 Inf

BA

VALOGNES

Montebourg

Merderet River

St. Germain

Les Dunes

XXX
US VIII

St. Sauveur

St. Mere-Eglise

XXX
US II

Ste-Marie-du-Mont

U

Barneville

Douve River

82 A/B

90 Inf

Vierville

Grandc

79 Inf

265 Inf

77 Inf

83 Inf

XXX

XXX

XXX

US XIX

Isigny

91 LL

CARENTAN

30 Inf

243 Inf

La Haye-du-Puits

17 SS PG

Taute River

Vire River

Miles   8

0

Kilometers   10

Lessey

Periers

XXX
LXXXIV

352 Inf

ST. LO

GENERAL
SITUATION
30 JUNE 1944

Marigny

XXX
II Fj

Coutances

XXXX
SEVENTH

K. WILKINS 86

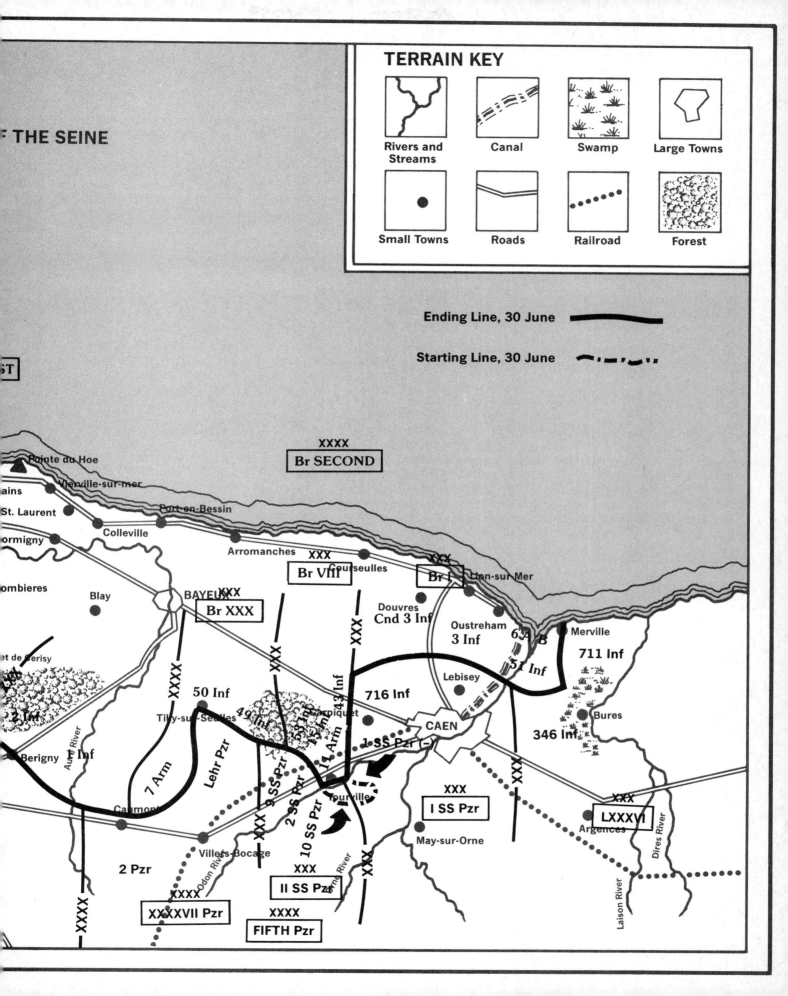

OF THE SEINE

TERRAIN KEY

Rivers and Streams	Canal
Swamp	Large Towns
Small Towns	Roads
Railroad	Forest

Ending Line, 30 June

Starting Line, 30 June

XXXX
Br SECOND

Pointe du Hoe

Vierville-sur-mer

St. Laurent

Port-en-Bessin

Colleville

rmigny

ombieres

Blay

Arromanches

XXX
Br VIII

Courseulles

XXX
Br I

Lion-sur Mer

BAYEUX

XXX
Br XXX

Douvres

Cnd 3 Inf

Oustreham
3 Inf

6 A B

Merville

et de Cerisy

XXX

XXX

XXXX

50 Inf

XXX

716 Inf

Lebisey

51 Inf

711 Inf

2 Inf

Tilly-sur-Seulles

49 Inf

43 Inf

Carpiquet

CAEN

Bures

346 Inf

Berigny

1 Inf

7 Arm

Lehr Pzr

9 SS Pzr

59 Inf

12 Arm

1 SS Pzr (-)

Carmont

2 SS Pzr

Tourville

XXX
I SS Pzr

May-sur-Orne

XXX
LXXXVI

Argences

Villers-Bocage

10 SS Pzr

Odon River

Orne River

2 Pzr

XXXX

XXX
II SS Pzr

XXXX
XXXXVII Pzr

XXXX
FIFTH Pzr

Laison River

Dives River

July 3, 1944 D + 27

VIII Corps jumped off on schedule, augmented by a division from VII Corps. The plan was for 90th Inf. Div. to attack Mont Castre, a hill which commanded the Contentin plain, while 82d Airborne would attack the Poterie Ridge north and northwest of la Haye-du-Puits and 79th Division would attack the Montgardon Ridge and Hill 121, west of the town. After taking the objective, 82d Airborne was to be replaced by the other divisions from VIII Corps and sent to England for rest and refitting. The results of the plan were to be disappointing.

The 90th had a particularly difficult time of it. Mont Castre commanded the whole area and the Germans used it to great advantage in bringing their artillery to bear. The situation was made even more difficult by the fact that rainfall in June had made the ground extremely wet, therby making it slow going even without German opposition.

A minor piece of satisfaction for the Allies (and embarrassment for the Germans) occurred in the British sector, though the British may not even have been aware it had occurred. The Germans had planned to send frogmen downstream to blow up bridges at Benouville in an attempt to isolate the British divisions east of the Orne. The first attempt, in the beginning of July had failed because the frogman ran into some sort of obstacle. For the second attempt, they decided to put the frogmen in further upstream, though this would lengthen the distance they would have to swim. Unfortunately for the Germans, this time the frogman assigned the detail overestimated the distance he had covered. He correctly attached his torpedo to the bridge he found. When the torpedo exploded, much to German chagrin, the wrong bridge blew up— the bridge at Herouville which the Allies had been trying to knock out for some time by aerial bombardment in order to hinder German resupply over the Orne.

U.S. 29th Division cemetery, July, 1944.

Tanks: Quality

Tanks were first introduced in World War I. However, by the outbreak of World War II they had changed in design from the lozenge and other bulky shapes used in World War I to a form which has basically been followed to the present. To many people, a tank is anything on tracks. It is not uncommon to see a newspaper photograph depicting a self-propelled artillery piece or armored personnel carrier labeled "tank." In the broadest sense, a tank has three major characteristics: steel armor thick enough to withstand small arms bullets (up to and including heavy machineguns), full tracks, and a central rotating turret equipped with the main armament, usually a cannon of some sort. The only major exception to this last to see extensive action was the U.S. M3 Grant tank which had a turret but had its main gun, a 75mm cannon, mounted on the right side. Its inability to engage targets on the left of the vehicle made it ineffective and the only reason why it saw any action at all is that its 75mm gun could knock out the German tanks of North Africa, while its armor was as thick as anything on the North African battlefield. Once its successor, the M4 Sherman, was fielded, the M3 quickly passed out of service.

In the first fighting, the Germans were still using the PzKpfw I, with its machineguns. But the Germans considered these obsolete even then and by 1944 all tanks had a fairly heavy cannon. In addition, some tanks had a co-axially mounted machinegun, which meant that it was mounted in the turret and was elevated and depressed using the same controls as was used to elevate and depress the main gun. Further, tanks usually had a turret-mounted machinegun for purposes of engaging enemy aircraft. Since the sights on these machineguns were not very precise, it is questionable how much ammunition was wasted firing in vain at enemy aircraft and how many were actually brought down. Still, it gave the tank commander something to do other than simply watch the enemy come at him with all guns blazing. Lastly, it was common to have a bow machinegun operated by a man who sat next to the driver.

Tank engagements were normally at fairly close range because no tanks had rangefinders. Range was estimated and the estimated range was used by the gunner to fire the first round. If the first round missed, the gunner would try to see where it struck and move his sights so that the apparent strike of the round was moved on top of the target, a technique known as "burst on target." Although many gunners became quite skilled at estimating the range accurately, hitting beyond 1000 meters was a good feat. More often engagements were at 500 meters and even less, which is why tank battles tended to be short, vicious affairs.

Throughout the war there was a constant design battle between putting on a big enough gun to knock out enemy tanks, putting enough armor on friendly tanks to avoid getting knocked out by enemy tanks, and having enough mobility, when all that was done, to move around the battlefield with some speed. A heavy tank might be wonderful in terms of survival on the battlefield but in muddy ground it could easily get mired and some of the largest tanks the Germans fielded at the end of the war couldn't use many of the bridges in Europe, because they were too heavy. The U.S. had an additional problem in tank design, specifically as it related to World War II—it had to consider the problem of shipping the tanks to Europe. As a result, the Sherman, which had many drawbacks, remained the main American tank throughout the war simply because it was compact and could be put in cargo ships in quantity. One solution to the mobility problem was wider tracks. This spread the tank's weight over more ground.

Another factor of significance, especially at this time, was the question of the slope of the armor, particularly frontal and turret armor. The greater the slope, the more effective armor an enemy round must penetrate, since the round is coming straight at the target. Moreover, with sloped armor, there is a tendency for shot rounds to skip off.

Most nations fielded a number of different kinds of tanks, based on their perception of the uses they wanted of them. The Americans basically broke their tanks into light tanks and medium tanks. The light tanks were used in reconnaissance roles and the medium tanks for almost everything else. The U.S. never really got into the heavy tank business. The British generally divided their tanks into infantry tanks and cruiser tanks. The infantry tank was usually heavily armored, heavily gunned and slow. It was designed to support infantry

vs. Quantity

advances. The cruiser tank was lighter armored and faster, designed to fulfill the old cavalry pursuit role.

The Germans did not make such a formal distinction in their tanks but generally had a mix in their divisions so that one battalion had a heavier tank than the other. When the war began, the PzKpfw III was the heaviest tank they had in significant production so one battalion would have the PzKpfw III and the others the PzKpfw I or II. As the PzKpfw IV came into production the III became the "light" battalion's tanks. When the Panther was produced, the PzKpfw IV was relegated to the "light" tank role. The heavier tanks, beyond the Panther, were not usually made part of a Panzer division. Instead, they were fielded in separate heavy tank battalions while the PzKpfw IV/Panther mix remained standard for the divisions.

Tanks during this period had two principle kinds of main gun ammunition: shot and high explosive (HE). Shot was simply a solid, kinetic energy round which relied on velocity to punch a hole in the enemy tank. HE was an impact-detonated high explosive round, quite suitable for use against light skinned vehicles such as half-tracks, or against bunkers, and could even be used in lieu of artillery by driving the tank up a steep incline so it could get the high altitude necessary to achieve ranges compatible with artillery. In addition, the Germans used a High Explosive Anti-Tank (HEAT) round. HEAT is a shaped charge which, upon impact, sets off a high speed jet which burns its way through armor. Unlike shot, which depends on its speed to

penetrate, and therefore loses effectiveness at greater ranges, HEAT is equally effective at all ranges and is only dependant on the size of the charge to determine how much armor it can penetrate. HEAT is more expensive and more difficult to manufacture than shot, which may be why the Allies didn't use it since their concern was quantity production. Finally, all tanks were capable of firing a white phosphorus (WP) round which was nominally intended to permit them to set up their own smokescreen but also had a splendid effect on wooden buildings.

Tank nomenclature can be most confusing. The U.S. had the most simple system. Before a tank was put into production, it was assigned the letter designation "T" and an arabic numeral, though that number might not remain the same when the production was approved. The precursor of the Sherman was the T6. A production model was assigned the letter "M" and an arabic numeral. The Sherman was officially the M4. As major modifications were accepted into production, the initial alphanumeric acquired a suffic "A" with another number indicating, in effect, how many major modifications had been adopted up to the time of that particular vehicle. The most widely used version of the Sherman was the M4A3. The basic M4 had a welded hull, the M4A1 had a cast hull. The M4A2 had a welded hull but twin General Motors diesel engines in place of the radial engine of the M4 and M4A1. The M4A3 had a welded hull and a Ford V-8 engine. Finally, if a given modification was put into production but

not formally accepted as a permanent modification, it was assigned yet another alphanumeric, preceded by the letter "E" (for "experimental"). Once the modification was accepted, it was normal to drop the last and either assign a new "A" number or, if the change was not considered significant enough, simply revert to the standard designation. One major exception was the M4A3E8. This experimental variant used a horizontal volute suspensions system (HVSS) rather than the vertical volute system used on all prior versions. In fact, this became standard for the 76mm gun version but popular usage retained the "Easy 8" designation long after the Army had reverted to the basic M4A3.

Not all major variations received either an "E" designation or an "A" designation. The initial Sherman was a short-barrelled 75mm gun tank but by the time the war ended, it had a long barrelled 76mm gun. However, this was an added feature on the M4A3E8 (which originally had a 75mm gun also). Though this more powerful gun was a major variation by anyone's standards, no appropriate modification was made in the designation to reflect that.

The assignment of names has been an off-again on-again thing with the Americans. The naming of tanks was never really official.

The German system of tank designation was more complex but, paradoxically, very clear once it was understood. As a test model, tanks were normally assigned an arbitrary number, prefixed by VK for Vollkettenkraftfahrzeug, or full tracked vehicle. The Tiger, in its

(continued on next page)

(continued from previous page)

experimental model, was the VK.3001. Upon adoption for production, it was assigned another number which uniquely identified the vehicles among Germany's armored vehicles. This was the Sonderkraftfahrzeug (literally, special motor vehicle or ordinance) number, abbreviated Sd Kfz. Since this number encompassed both wheeled and tracked vehicles, armored and unarmored, tanks were given a further designation of Panzerkampfwagen (armored fighting vehicle), usually expressed with a Roman numeral. Although the German half-tracks were generally known by their Sd Kfz numbers, tanks were usually referred to by their PzKpwf numbers. PzKpfw I through IV were normally without names. From the PzKpfw V (Panther) on, the name was an integral part of the designation. Major variants were known by the designation "Ausfuhrung" (Ausf) and given a letter designation. To further designate a tank, it was not uncommon to describe the gun, normally expressed in centimeters. Since there were different purposes ascribed to guns, a tank gun, technically, was known as a Kampfwagenkanon or KwK. Further, it was not uncommon to express the length of the gun barrel in terms of calibers (in other words, how many times the diameter of the barrel the gun was long). Therefore, one might see the production Tiger designated as PzKpfw VI Tiger Ausf E (Sd Kfz 182), 8.8cm KwK L/56. The designation of barrel length is not merely idle information. In general, given the same calibre gun, the longer gun will have the higher muzzle velocity and therefore can penetrate more enemy armor, using shot.

There were exceptions to the use of Roman numerals to designate tanks and that was in the case of foreign tanks taken into German service. Perhaps the most famous of these was the PzKpfw 38(t), which was the Czech TNHP (LT 38) taken into German service after the occupation of the balance of Czechoslovakia in 1939. The letter in parentheses designated the original country of origin (in this case "t" for "Tschechoslowakische" or "Czechoslovakian"). The Germans used the PzKpfw 35R(f) in the

Tanks

Comparative Data of Principal Tanks

PzKpfw IV Ausf H (Sd Kfz 161)—Germany

Speed:	24–38 km/h
Range:	210–320 km
Main Gun:	75mm KwK 40 L/48
Secondary:	1 turret mg; 1 bow mg
Armor:	hull—80 mm; turret—30mm
Weight:	25 tons
Comments:	Largely outdated by D-Day due to inadequate turret armor and straight armor. It was the workhorse of the German panzer force for the majority of the war. The better tanks were never made in enough quantity to replace the PzKpfw IV

PzKpfw V Ausf G Panther (Sd Kfz 171)—Germany

Speed:	25–46 km/h
Range:	100–200 km
Main Gun:	75mm KwK 42 L/70
Secondary:	7.92mm turret mg; 7.92mm coax mg; 7.92 bow mg
Armor:	hull—80mm; turret—110mm
Weight:	44.8 tons
Comments:	Arguably the best tank of the war, with only the Russian T34 giving it any competition. Had power traverse for turret.

PzKpfw VI Ausf E Tiger(H) (Sd Kfz 181)—Germany

Speed:	19–37 km/h
Range:	67–117 km
Main Gun:	88mm KwK 36 L/56
Secondary:	7.92mm coax mg; 7.92 bow mg
Armor:	hull—100mm; turret—110mm
Weight:	57 tons
Comments:	With its thick armor, the Tiger was a tough tank to kill. Its 88mm gun made it the most deadly tank of the war. Slow power traverse made it hard to engage the enemy from unexpected directions before they could get the Tiger turret turned. Mechanically not very reliable and hard to fix.

PzKpfw VI Ausf B Königstiger (Sd. Kfz 182)—Germany

Speed:	24 km/h
Range:	106 km
Main Gun:	88mm KwK 43 L/71
Secondary:	7.92mm turret mg; 7.92 coax mg; 7.92 bow mg
Armor:	hull—150mm; turret—100mm
Weight:	66 tons
Comments:	Just fielded around the time of D-Day. Also known as Tiger II. Heavy armor made it difficult to knock out. Slow. Too heavy for some bridges. Excellent armor configuration, with few vertical, straight surfaces. All of the mechanical problems of the Tiger and then some. The heaviest tank ever in production, including modern tanks.

M4A3 Sherman—United States

Speed:	48 km/h
Range:	193 km
Main Gun:	75mm L/40
Secondary:	.50 cal turret mg; .30 cal coax mg; .30 cal bow mg
Armor:	62mm
Weight:	33.8 tons
Comments:	A most controversial tank. Known as the "Ronson" to the Germans because it caught on fire easily. Not especially well armored. Its 75mm gun was adequate for the PzKpfw IV but had trouble with the Panther and especially the Tiger. A powered turret made it able to engage multiple targets. Very reliable mechanically. Basic hull design made it easy to manufacture. Rear engine with front drive made it unnecessarily tall. Had a stabilized gun to permit firing on the move, and power traverse.

M5A1 Stuart—United States

Speed:	58 km/h cross country; 90 km/h road
Range:	160 km
Main Gun:	37mm L/53
Secondary:	.30 cal turret mg; .30 cal coax mg; .30 cal bow mg
Armor:	51mm
Weight:	16.5 tons
Comments:	Standard light tank of U.S. Army. Widely used by British in North Africa. Had a stabilized gun with power traverse. Inadequate for regular tank battles. Excellent in recon role. Range was its limitation.

A27(M), Cruiser Mark VIII, Cromwell IV—Great Britain

Speed:	61 km/h
Range:	130–280 km
Main Gun:	75mm L/40
Secondary:	1 coax mg, 1 bow mg
Armor:	76mm
Weight:	28 tons
Comments:	Introduced in Normandy. High mobility made it excellent for breakthrough operations. Saw service into Korea.

Infantry Tank Mark IV, Churchill III—Great Britain

Speed:	25 km/h
Range:	193 km
Main Gun:	6 pdr L/52
Secondary:	1 coax mg, 1 bow mg
Armor:	88mm
Weight:	39.2 tons
Comments:	The best of the infantry tanks. Originally designed to break through a World War I type front expected to develop between the French Maginot Line and the German West Wall. Not up to the speeds of 1944 tank operations. Many were adapted for special purpose vehicles for invasion of Normandy.

A17E2 Mark VII Light Tank, Tetrarch—Great Britain

Speed:	
Range:	
Main Gun:	2 pdr, L/52
Secondary:	
Armor:	
Weight:	
Comments:	Principal British light tank. The Hamilcar glider was developed to lift this tank to the battlefield.

initial defense at Normandy, which was their designation for the French Renault 1935 tank. In Russia they made use of Russian tanks, especially as chassis for various uses.

British writings sometimes refer to the pre-Panther tanks as "Mark IV" or the like. Strictly speaking they did not use their numerical designations the way the British did their "mark" system.

The British system is probably the hardest to sort out but for the common practice of simply referring to a tank by its name. In fact, they had the widest array of tanks of any army during the war. The cruiser tanks were all initially known by alphanumerics similar in concept to the U.S. system. However, instead of an "M" for an initial letter, the model was designated "A" with a number and variant "E" with a number. The Tetrarch light tank was officially the A17E2. Even some infantry tanks got into this designation system. The Churchill was the A22E1 (but the Churchill VII, which saw action in Normandy, was the A22F). Then, too, some tanks were simply known by a Mark number. The Covenanter I was officially the Mark V Cruiser. The infantry tanks, by contrast, were generally simply known by a name with a Roman numeral indicating the variant. The Valentine, mainstay of the desert war, was originally a variant on the A10E3, became an infantry tank under the name Infantry Tank Mark III, became known as the Valentine I and from Valentine III through XI, had no other designation than the name and number. U.S. tanks made a considerable contribution to the British tank force and were adopted using similar designations—the name and a Roman numeral. One of the toughest variants on the Sherman was the Sherman Vc (Firefly) with a 17 pounder gun.

Identification of British vehicles is made more complicated for people not familiar with the British system by their practice of designating guns as 2 pounders, 3 pounders, etc. The standard British gun sizes, with their metric equivalents, are: 2 pdr = 40mm; 3 pdr = 47mm; 6 pdr = 57mm; 17 pdr = 76.2mm.

July 4, 1944 D + 28

Disappointed with the results obtained by VIII Corps during the first day of the attack, Bradley hoped that VII Corps, back in the line from its success in taking Cherbourg, would show the same fire it had previously demonstrated. New to VII Corps was the 83d Division, which had replaced the 101st Airborne in the middle of June. Collins hoped that the 83d could make three kilometers the first day. The VII Corps front was so narrow where it was starting its attack, that only the 83d could be put up on line. However, with the three kilometers he wanted the 83d to gain, he could then insert the veteran 4th Inf. Div. The Germans had taken good advantage of the adverse conditions off the roads. Knowing that tracked vehicles could barely move off the roads and wheels, such as the trucks needed to tow artillery, would never be able to operate across country until it dried out from the June rains, the Germans commanded all of the key roads and road junctions. The 83d did not gain more than a few hundred meters on July 4 and lost almost 1400 men. VIII Corps was still inching along and there was some concern that perhaps the 90th Inf. Div. needed a new commander again. Only the 82d Airborne made any progress in this sector, averaging two kilometers a day.

The same day the British launched the Canadian 3d Infantry Division in Operation Windsor, designed to gain control of both the village and airfield of Carpiquet, west of Caen. The lead element was the Canadian 8th Inf. Bde, composed of three battalions, the Queen's Own Rifles of Canada, the North Shore Rgt, from New Brunswick, and the French-Canadian Le Régiment de la Chaudière. The 7th Brigade added the Royal Winnipeg Rifles. Supporting the brigade were the tanks of the Fort Garry Horse, more prosaically known as the 10th Arm. Rgt, out of the Canadian 2d Arm. Bde, as well as the Crab tanks—Shermans with a rotating drum of chain flails to clear minefields—and Crocodiles—Churchill tanks converted to flamethrowers—from the British 79th Arm. Div. In addition, the Canadians received massive artillery support in the form of 428 guns as well as naval gunnery from *HMS Rodney,* with her 16" guns, and the monitor *Roberts,* with 15" guns.

Against this massive force was approximately 150 members of *25th SS-Panzergrenadier Rgt,* part of the *12th SS-Pzr Div.,* with a few tanks and some 88's. The Germans were able to have some idea what was afoot by monitoring radio traffic. Even when code words and other devices are used to conceal the true meaning of radio traffic, the mere volume can give a good idea what is going on. A major increase in radio traffic generally indicates a major operation and that is exactly what the Germans detected coming from the radios of the Canadian 3d Division. In fact, on the morning of July 4, the Germans detected enough traffic to suspect that the attack forces were beginning to move. They calculated, based on past experience, that the attack was likely to begin at 0700 and accordingly called for artillery and mortar fire on the suspected assembly positions at 0600. Listening on their radios, the Germans also determined that these "preemptive" shellings had drawn blood.

The Chaudière regiment had the lead in trying to take the village. Only 50 Germans defended the village itself, but they made the Canadians pay a steep price for taking it, with house-to-house fighting the rule.

The German artillery was so intense that the Queen's Own Rifles could not take the control building for the airfield. Even after dark, when they tried to put out a defensive minefield, German shelling inflicted so many casualties that the effort was abandoned.

American soldier poses with two French girls, July 9th.

July 5, 1944 D + 29

All along the front, July 5 looked like a bad re-run of July 4. The Canadians were subjected to further artillery fire and were still unsuccessful in efforts to take the airfield.

By the 5th, the 82d Airborne had achieved its objective in taking the Poterie hills, to the north of le Haye-du-Puits. They may have had a special incentive since, after that, they were scheduled to be replaced by the 79th and 90th and sent back to England for the same kind of rehabilitation the 101st was already enjoying. The 82d needed it, having been steadily worn down by the fighting to the point that it was under 50% strength. The 325th Glider Rgt, for example, had only 33% of its strength left. For the rest of the attacking American divisions, success still eluded them. The 90th was particularly bothered by the German occupation of Mont Castre, which allowed them to harrass every move the division made through well-directed artillery fire. The result was that the Americans became frustrated and instead of co-ordinating operations would lash out without any coordination or simply hold back, two conditions which did not exist in the more experienced 82d Airborne and which allowed the 82d to succeed where 90th was unable to. The one thing which probably saved the 90th Division from getting a third commander was the fact that the 79th, which had performed so well in the race to Cherbourg, was doing no better here. The 79th, like the 90th, was averaging less than a kilometer a day advance.

In VIII Corps area, the 83d managed to inch forward some more, to the tune of another 750 casualties, to give it a net gain for two days of 1.5 kilometers.

On the German side, another commander

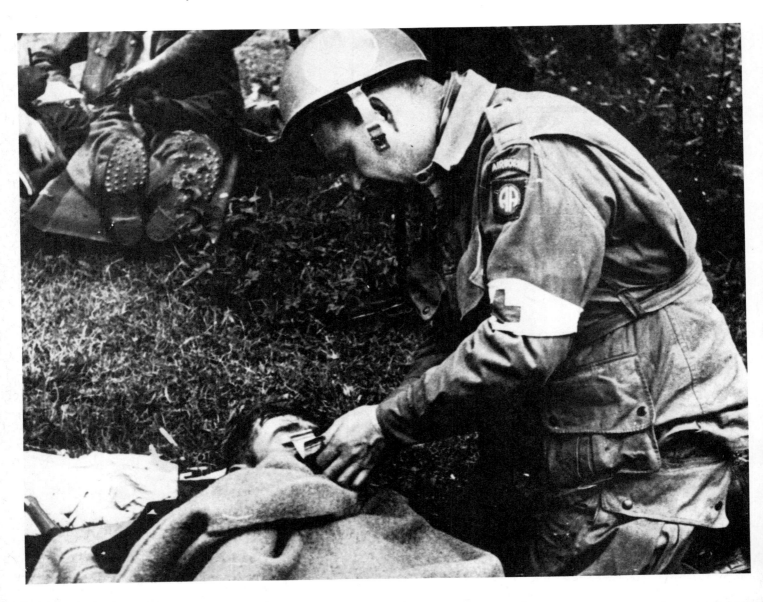

was relieved. This time it was the lot of Geyr von Schweppenburg, who had the bad taste to criticize the way the defense was being handled on a strategic level. He was replaced by the more pliable General der Panzertruppe, Heinrich Eberbach.

Left: *82nd Airborne medical officer, July 12. The fibre liner inside the steel helmet is clearly visible as are the special paratroopers' pockets on jacket and trousers. Metal buttons and hobnails on soldier at top left probably identify a German prisoner.*

Below: *Captured German NCO tagged for identification, July 30.*

U.S. soldiers under sniper fire, July 6th. Soldier at center has grenade launcher fitted to his rifle. The bocage country could reduce visibility to a few feet.

July 6, 1944 D + 30

Celebrating one month on the continent must have been frustrating in Allied headquarters. The Canadians were still battering themselves bloody against the determined handful of defenders from the *12th SS-Panzer Division* around Carpiquet airfield. Worse, the airfield had actually been held by Canadian troops on June 6 but abandoned when it became apparent that they could not get enough troops forward to maintain a foothold. In the ensuing 29 days, they had not been able to regain that original piece of ground.

The fighting around the airfield was inconclusive on this date. While several German counterattacks were repelled, the Canadians could not gain ground themselves. However, on a dark note, word had filtered back that some Canadians, captured the previous day, had simply been shot by the SS. On the 6th an advance patrol from the *12th SS-Panzer* had infiltrated the forward positions of the Chaudière. When they were captured vengeance was taken. Quite literally, throats were slit and no prisoners were taken. The incidents of these few days colored the relationship between the Canadians and the Germans—especially the Waffen-SS—for the rest of the war. On the German side the word was that the Canadians didn't take prisoners and from the Canadian side, the memory of the Waffen-SS's treatment of its Canadian prisoners tended to make the Canadians less willing to give quarter.

In the American attack, the small gains of the 83d over the previous two days were enough to allow the 4th Inf. Div. to go back in. By this point, Collins revised his estimate and hoped to reach Sainteny, the original first day objective, by the end of the 7th. However the 4th was no more successful than the 83d and the units inched forward both in VII Corps and VIII Corps sector.

One point which was slowly beginning to tell, was the effect of the intensity of the fighting. The losses of the 82d Airborne since they landed have already been noted. The 4th Infantry had lost 5,400 casualties since D-Day. However, it had received 4,400 replacements. While still well below strength, the fact that four fifths of the losses had been replaced put it—and other Allied divisions—in a far better state than the Germans. For the Germans there were very few replacements.

CHAPTER VII

THE FALL OF CAEN AND ST. LÔ
July 7, 1944 D+31

It rained again on July 7, adding to the ground water which was already making the American attack move at a crawl. It also forced cancellation of an air strike aimed at opening the way for VII Corps to take Sainteny. More significantly, the Germans moved *2d Pz Div* "Das Reich" from the British sector to face VII Corps, adjacent to *17th SS-Panzergrenadier.*

July 7 was the date for XIX Corps to add its weight to the attack. XIX Corps had been in the line since June 12 but had no major role until now. It had a more difficult task than the other two corps. The 30th Inf. Div., on its east flank, had to cross a difficult obstacle at the outset—the Vire et Taute Canal and the Vire River. The canal was fordable but the river was eighteen meters wide in places and between 2.5 and 4 meters deep. This required bridges or, until they were built, boats. Initially, they expected considerable opposition since elements of *17th SS-Panzergrenadier* and *275th* and *352d Infantry Divisions* were reported in the division's path. However, the VII Corps attacks had drawn away much of the potential resistance with the result that the 30th got across both river and canal with relative ease. This was aided by a heavy artillery barrage hitting all buildings suspected of hiding German troops and then a rolling barrage in front of the advancing Americans. The artillery was effective, minimizing the effect of not getting an air strike, which had been scrubbed for the same reason as VII Corps didn't get its strike—the rain.

Because the crossings went so well, Bradley decided to put the U.S. 3d Arm. Div. into the bridgehead. This would be the first full commitment of an armored division in the American sector. A combat command of 3d Armored had been used by V Corps earlier—sustaining serious casualties. Now the whole division was to pass through 30th Infantry.

However, because the situation which permitted the 3d Armored to be thrown into the fight had developed without warning, there was little time for preparation. At this point only one bridge was available for crossing the Vire. Moving the tanks of an armored unit requires more coordination of road space than moving troops on foot—as the British had found out at Cheux during Operation Epsom. Further, the 30th was using the same bridge to move its people across and there were considerable numbers of short tempers for the rest of the day. The 3d Armored had not completed moving across the Vire when the 7th of July came to an end.

In the British sector, July 7 was marked by a massive bombing raid on Caen. Some 450 heavy bombers of Bomber Command attacked in an attempt to disrupt the German defenses in front of Caen. Montgomery had planned a major attack to try to take Caen head on. Once Carpiquet was taken, he planned to launch three divisions directly into Caen, doing the kind of set piece battle for which he had established a reputation. Having found at Carpiquet that the Germans had established a formidable defensive belt around the city, the plan was modified to enlist the aid of the RAF. The idea had already been used by Maj. Gen. Collins when Carentan was still in German hands—bomb it heavily and then, while the enemy was still in shock, charge in to take it. The difficulty here was that the bombing was to occur in the early evening of the 7th but the attack would not begin until the morning of the 8th.

A major consideration was that the planes to be used, the same kinds of strategic bombers used to attack Hamburg, Berlin, the Ruhr and other targets in Germany, were not normally concerned with pinpoint accuracy. In laying down a swathe of bombs, if a few planes miss their aiming point by a few kilometers, there is

U.S. Stuart high tank moves through French village, July 27th. The late-war tank had a lower turret and better armor than the Stuart "Honey" used in North Africa.

no major problem—especially if the target is strictly enemy territory. Moreover, there was a natural tendency for self-preservation among bomber crews. Once the Flak started coming up, they tended to become quite "approximate" in their accuracy, preferring to drop their bombs in the vicinity and get out of harm's way. Further, while British bombers had good bombsights, they did not have the precision and accuracy of the Norden Bombsight which allowed American bombers to make daylight raids against Germany. As a result, Air Chief Marshal Harris, who headed bomber command, insisted on a six km safety buffer between the British front lines and the aiming point. In reality, that alone should have caused the cancellation of the raid because the Germans and British were so close together that a six km stand-off from the British lines ensured that no bombs would hit the German forward defensive positions. At best it would disrupt the German rearward communications. However, bombers had proven a dramatic weapon. The kind of destruction wrought in Germany made for spectacular photographs and there was a tendency, given the number of bombers available, to use them, even if they might not be as effective as desired.

For all of these reasons, the aiming point became Caen itself and Caen managed to get 2,500 tons of bombs dropped on it, commencing around 2150. In effect, it was the first effort at what came to be known as "carpet bombing." The area to be attacked was a strip four km wide and 1.5 km deep. The sole effect of the raid was the virtual destruction of Caen. Though the target was supposed to be the Germans, the only casualties were French. The city was reduced to rubble, which ensured that the British would have a hard time gettting through the city. It was not a glorious moment in the liberation of Europe.

The slow going, especially around Caen, was beginning to fray nerves. The American press was becoming particularly critical of Montgomery's lack of progress, which they attributed to nothing more than poor leadership. Montgomery's personality didn't help. He was personally resentful that he had not been given over-all command of Overlord and although he was the commander on the ground right now, he knew that once Third Army was activated in France, Bradley would become an Army Group Commander in his own right and out from under Montgomery's control. There was also a tendency on Montgomery's part to come across to Americans as though he were a teacher dealing with slightly retarded students.

Things reached a point where Eisenhower felt it necessary to write a letter to Montgomery suggesting that efforts on the British side had not been all out and that this was permitting the Germans to build up their defenses. He noted, with some accuracy, that the British had never launched a full-scale assault in the British sector. Churchill had already let Brooke know he was disenchanted with Montgomery. Churchill's concern was that if they didn't break out of Normandy fairly quickly, they might see a repetition of the position warfare which bled Britain and France white in World War I. As a result, pressure began to grow to replace Montgomery unless something dramatic happened.

The results of the next two operations, Charnwood and Goodwood, took some of the steam out of that drive. Ironically, the best evidence is that these operations were undertaken without particular regard for satisfying the critics at home. If Montgomery's attitude suggested that he always thought he was right, that same attitude caused him to turn a blind eye toward his critics. He did what he felt was correct, regardless of the consequences, being content to let the results, in the end, speak for themselves.

Montgomery's ultimate problem was that he was legitimately concerned that he did not have the manpower available for a full-scale assault using all of the forces at his command. The Americans were taking substantial casualties in their fighting but they had the manpower reserves to replace these losses. The British didn't. Perhaps the worst legacy of World War I was the loss of manpower.

July 8, 1944   D + 32

For the better part of the 8th, 3d Arm. Div. struggled to gets its lead element, Combat Command B, across the single bridge it had to share with the 30th Infantry Division. If Maj. Gen. Hobbs, the commander of the 30th, thought that, once through, CCB would run interference ahead of his division, he was disappointed. As soon as they were across, 3d Arm. Div. Commander Maj. Gen. Watson directed CCB to turn south on unimproved roads and trails, following the banks of the Vire River. Bitter experience in June, when CCB had spent some time in the line, showed that the Germans had solid command of the main road and that the only way to get around them without heavy losses, was to go across country as well as make use of the side roads. The problem was that on the west bank of the Vire the hedgerows were especially numerous, which made any cross-country movement very slow.

With his passage blocked and CCB making little progress, Hobbs advised the corps commander that he wanted nothing further to do with the tanks. Corlett informed him that since the tanks were available he would have to use them and went so far as to put CCB under operational control of 30th Inf. Div. as the day drew to a close.

For the rest of this drive to crack through the bocage, the Americans were equally unsuccessful all along the front. To replace 82d Airborne, Maj. Gen. Middleton, commanding VIII Corps, decided to put the 8th Inf. Div. into the line in the middle of his corps. The 8th was another new division in the sense that it had not seen combat, though it had been part of the prewar regular army. Despite a reputation of being one of the best-trained divisions to come into the area, the 8th had the same kinds of problems which plagued the other divisions in their first efforts in combat.

The British began yet another drive to seize Caen. Called Operation Charnwood, it committed the 59th Division to combat in the center, the 3d Division to the east of the Canadian 3d to the west. They were backed up by the special tanks of the 79th Armoured and two Canadian armoured brigades.

The Germans had not only not been touched by the prior evening's bombardment, but the bombing had served to put them on full alert, so that when the attack jumped off at 0420, no surprise was achieved. The British and Canadians on the flanks made considerable headway,

as might be expected from experienced units, while the 59th, in the center, moved much more slowly. The Canadians made enough progress that they were soon able to pass on the other side of the defenders of Carpiquet, leaving them between the Canadian 8th Brigade, which had made the initial attack earlier, and the remainder of the division now passing to their east.

From the VIII Corps, the 43d (Wessex) was sent to try to take Hill 112 again—the same Hill 112 which had proven impossible to hold during Operation Epsom.

An army travels on its feet? British and American troops during a lighter moment earlier in the war. The long campaign to break out of Normandy created strains between the Allies.

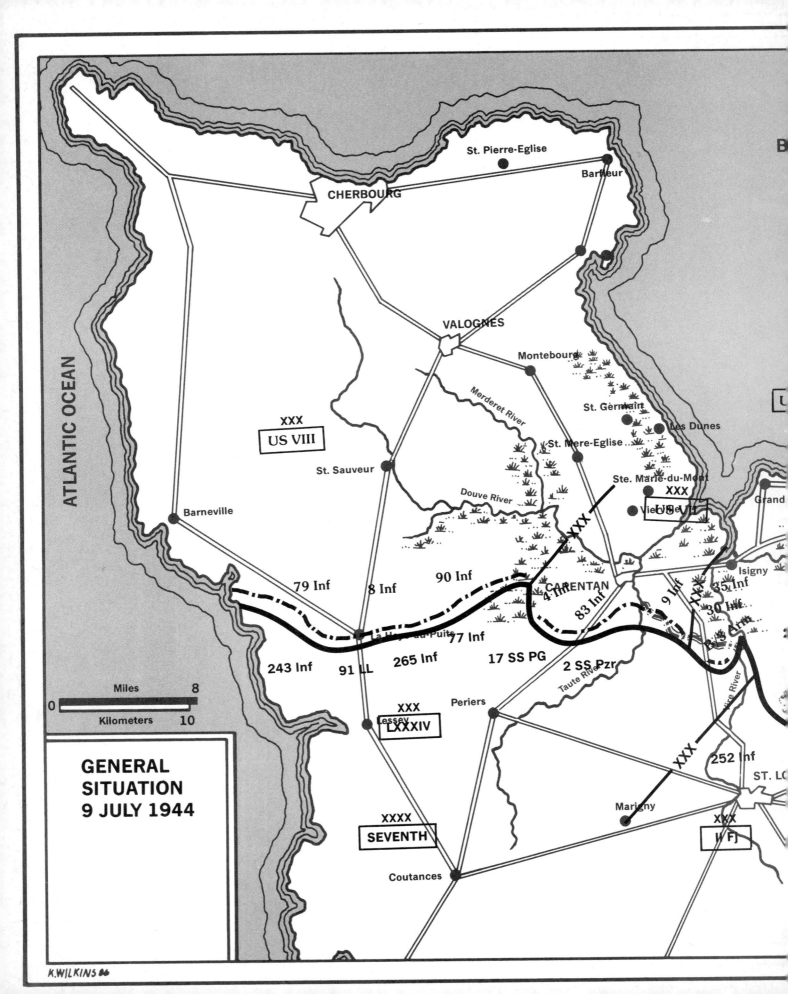

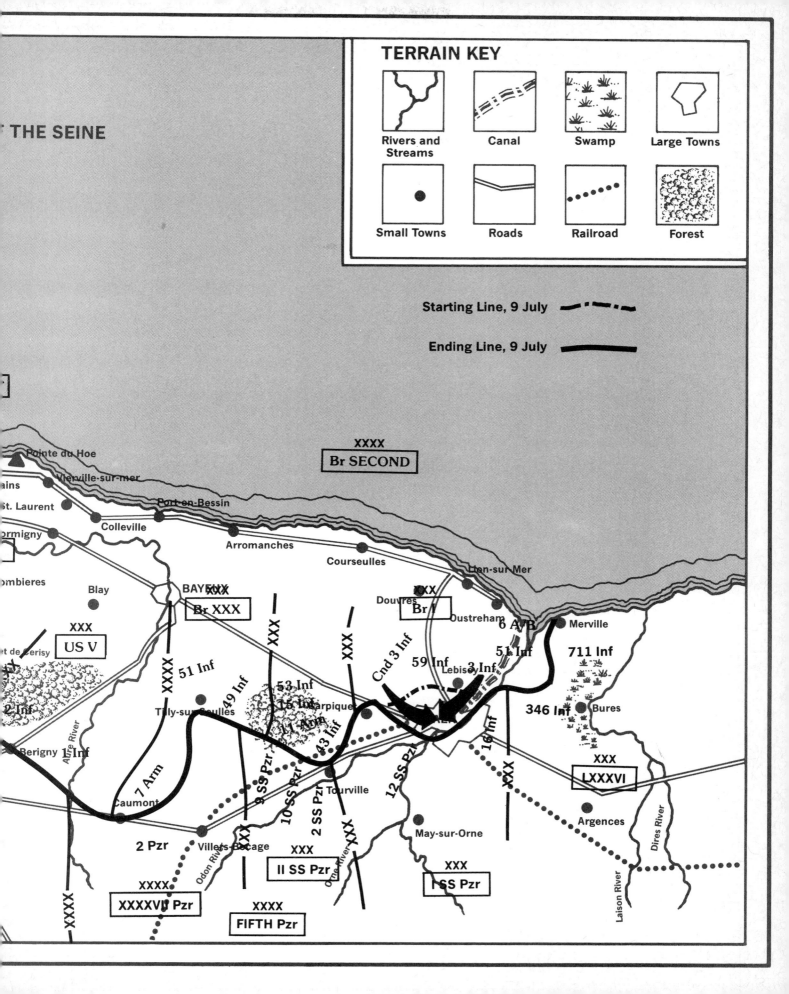

THE SEINE

TERRAIN KEY

Rivers and Streams	Canal	Swamp	Large Towns
Small Towns	Roads	Railroad	Forest

Starting Line, 9 July

Ending Line, 9 July

XXXX
Br SECOND

Pointe du Hoe
Vierville-sur-mer
ains
St. Laurent
Port-en-Bessin
Colleville
ormigny
Arromanches
Courseulles
Lion-sur-Mer
ombieres
Blay
BAYEUX
XXX
Br XXX
Douvres
XXX
Br I
Oustreham
6 A/B
Merville
711 Inf
XXX
US V
t de Cerisy
XXXX 51 Inf
59 Inf
Cnd 3 Inf
Lebisey
3 Inf
51 Inf
346 Inf
Bures
2 Inf
49 Inf
53 Inf
15 Inf
Tilly-sur-Seulles
arpiquet
11 Arm
43 Inf
16 Inf
Berigny 1 Inf
Alle River
7 Arm
9 SS Pzr
10 SS Pzr
2 SS Pzr
Tourville
12 SS Pzr
XXX
LXXXVI
Caumont
Argences
Dires River
2 Pzr
Villers-Bocage
Odon River
II SS Pzr
Orne River
May-sur-Orne
I SS Pzr
Laison River
XXXX
XXXXVII Pzr
XXXX
FIFTH Pzr

July 9, 1944   D + 33

Seeing that the line which the *12th SS-Panzer* was holding was really beyond the ability of the weakened division to hold, the commander, SS-Oberführer Kurt Meyer sought permission on the 8th to fall back to the river, which ran through Caen. However this request was denied because of Hitler's order that every inch of ground must be held. Finally, without orders, on the 9th Meyer ordered his men to fall back. The Canadian 3d and British 3d entered Caen that day from the west and east respectively. By the end of the day, they had secured Caen north of the Orne but could not get across.

By now, VIII Corps was in La Haye-du-Puits, which put them well behind their planned timetable. Still, Corlett looked to expand the operation and put the 9th Inf. Div. back of the line, east of the Taute River, to threaten the German flank there. The hope was that this would open up things for VII Corps. The corps boundary between the VII and XIX Corps was the Taute River and the 9th, which was a VII Corps unit, would be operating in the XIX Corps area. Accordingly, Bradley moved the corps boundary so that 9th Infantry would remain part of VII Corps.

July 10, 1944 D + 34

Still trying to get around Caen, the British sent the 43d (Wessex) Division against Hill 112, the high watermark of the earlier Epsom operation, augmenting the division with the 46th (Highland) Brigade out of the Canadian 3d Inf. Div. as well as the British 4th Armoured and 31st Tank Brigades. The attack, which jumped off at 0500, was dubbed Operation Jupiter. Because the Germans also recognized the importance of Hill 112, they had given its defense to the *502 Ind. SS Heavy Tank Battalion.* This was another Tiger battalion and ensured that the fighting would be stiff.

The British got as far as Maltot before the Tigers moved into action. Not surprisingly, the British tanks got the worst of the fight as the thick armor of the Tigers allowed them to withstand the British anti-tank rounds. By nightfall, the British decided to send the 5th Battalion, the Duke of Cornwall's Light Infantry up Hill 112 to stabilize the situation. The Germans also decided to send some Tigers to Hill 112 for the same purpose. When 5th DCLI passed through the 129th Brigade, they were met by the German force coming up the other side. The situation for the British got so bad that they fired a smokescreen to allow themselves cover in order to pull back. The Tigers pressed on through the smoke and got to the other side, where they found they were right on top of the retreating British. Just as they began the slaughter, they received orders to fall back themselves, sparing the British even worse carnage. The fighting was not over, however. The Germans were to nickname the hill "Kalverienberg"—"Mount Calvary"—before the fighting was done.

Things were not going any better for the Americans at Hauts-Vents. The tanks which had spent the night on the hill, unmolested, pulled off in the morning to rejoin their unit. Now CCB had the task of retaking the hill. Col. Roysdon, who had replaced Brig. Gen. Bohn when Hobbs lost patience with him, in his own turn became the object of Hobbs' wrath because he was not moving fast enough to suit Hobbs.

The problem for CCB was that *Panzer Lehr* had finally arrived in the area, moving up from the British sector when it became apparent that the Americans had a major push underway. Although there were nominally a number of divisions fighting the Americans, they had been engaged almost from the start of the Allied landings and were reduced in strength, many could field nothing like the resources of a division. The main German advantage was the tremendous advantage the defenders had in the bocage. In addition, *Panzer Lehr* arrived to provide a valuable bolster to the German defenses. More important to the day's activities, they arrived in time to lay down a fierce mortar and artillery barrage, forcing CCB off Hill 91 late in the day.

July 11, 1944 D + 35

CCB attacked again on the morning of the 11th and was thrown back again. That afternoon Col. Roysdon personally led yet another attack which carried the hill once more. This time the Americans were there to stay. *Panzer Lehr* had planned to launch a counterattack to take St. Jean-de-Daye but the bocage helped the defenders, in this case the Americans. *Panzer Lehr* made some initial penetrations along the boundary between two of the regiments of the 9th Inf. Div. as well as the boundary between the 9th and the 30th, but *Panzer Lehr*'s records reflect that it lost about 25% of its effective combat strength in the day's fighting.

*Typical scene in bocage
illustrates how suited the
country was for snipers,
ambushes, and booby traps.*

In the meantime, Bradley had decided to try to secure St. Lô and for that purpose the 2d Inf. Div., from V Corps, and the 29th, from XIX Corps began attacking toward St. Lô. The 2d had drawn to within a few kilometers of the city in June during the drive to Caumont. In fact, one key piece of terrain, Hill 192, had been in American hands but the 2d had not retained it at the time because the Americans were not ready to make a push on St. Lô just then. Now they had to regain it and do so against the tough *3d Fallschirm Division*. In contrast to what was going on elsewhere, the 2d did this despite several aspects of the plans going wrong.

For the 29th Inf. Div., their first goal was the Martinville Ridge. Once that was secured, they would turn to the west and head toward Martinsville and St. Lô. This task would be handled by the 116th RCT and because that turn would force them to run parallel to the German positions, exposing their left flank to German fire, it was the most dangerous aspect of the 29th operation. When they did attack, they reached the Martinsville Ridge on the 11th but as they made their turn, the anticipated casualties began. The regiment lost 500 in the first day.

For the British, the agony on Hill 112 was far from over. The hill changed hands again and again on the 11th as both sides fought to keep this key piece of terrain from falling into the other's permanent control.

The British were working on yet another attack, this one involving their left, or easternmost, flank. The 51st Highland and 6th Airborne Divisions had been sitting east of the Orne, almost forgotten since their duels with the *21st Panzer* and *Kampfgruppe Luck* in the first few days. Named Goodwood, this operation was scheduled to start a week away. With only half of Caen in British hands, they were still in no position to get out into the better tank country beyond Caen. In ironic fulfillment of Montgomery's objective of drawing more German attention to the British than the American side, every fresh panzer unit to arrive went in first on the British side. July 11 saw the arrival of yet another heavy tank battalion, this one being the *503d*. The *503d* was not an SS battalion, but did bring along one company of the superheavy Königstiger. If the Tiger was hard to knock out, the Königstiger was harder.

U.S. artillery bombards
Carentan, July 11.

July 12, 1944 D + 36

Having repelled *Panzer Lehr,* 9th Inf. Div. was able to begin moving on its own attack. In XIX Corps's operation against St. Lô, Maj. Gen. Gerhardt, the commander of the 29th Inf. Div., tried to pass 175th RCT through the 116th to bolster the attack but German artillery proved especially troublesome with another 500 casualties being sustained.

For the British, planning on Goodwood went on—as did the fighting on Hill 112. By this point the hill top was barren of trees—only charred stumps remained. That and wrecks of Tiger and Churchill tanks, as well as bodies from both sides.

Baking biscuits during a lull in the fighting, July 13th.

July 13, 1944 D + 37

In the case of the 8th Inf. Div., firing the commander seemed to work. The division began a series of lateral movements, slipping off to the side of German resistance, and started advancing. At the same time, the 79th and 90th were also beginning to advance—not rapidly but steadily. The price was still steep. For example, during the first six weeks in combat the 90th Inf. Div. had a replacement rate among officers of 150%, and over 100% among enlisted men. Other divisions lost in similar proportion. Only the prodigious American build-up prior to D-Day allowed the steady flow of replacements which, in turn, allowed the Americans to keep up the pressure. The Germans, deprived of similar replacement, were forced to husband their strength. Again, the bocage was their strongest ally because they could put one man in a hedgerow and hold off a much larger American force.

In the 29th Inf. Div. operation, the 175th RCT, which had moved through the 116th RCT to the south, attempted an attack on the new German positions running along the Martinville Ridge, but was generally unsuccessful. This brought a revision of thinking at corps and division level. The objective was St. Lô and there was no sound military reason to try indirect approaches if a direct one would work. The approach from the east was getting stalled so Corlett tried the direct approach from the north, using 35th Infantry Division.

For the British, Hill 112 was still in German hands. For the German Panzergrenadiers Hill 112 was simply a large killing ground as the British artillery worked its deadly business among them.

July 14, 1944 D + 38

Bastille Day saw the VIII Corps finally secure the Ayr River line. The 79th Division was on the Ayr estuary, the 8th, still in the center, on a ridgline overlooking the Ayr, and the 90th had reached the Seves River and made contact with VII Corps. The twelve days of fighting had gained a bare eleven kilometers of ground at the cost of 10,000 casualties. They were only one-third of the way to the original objective which was the high ground of the Coutances-St. Lô ridge.

At this rate, the Americans would never get out of the bocage. Even before the 14th, the Americans had been at work on a solution to the problem—Operation Cobra, a steady drive down the Cotentin Peninsula through la Haye-du-Puits and Périers to Coutances and then to Avranches, where they would break out into Britanny.

As part of the plan, the corps boundaries were shifted so that VII Corps shifted eastward, picking up 30th Inf. Div. in the process from XIX Corps. These two divisions would spearhead the attack, followed by 2d and 3d Arm. and 1st Inf. Divs. The start point was to be the St. Lô—Periers road. This would be carried out by both VII and XIX Corps and involved the capture of St. Lô to secure the St. Lô—Periers road at its eastern terminus. Bradley hoped to be in position to launch Cobra by July 20.

U.S. 105 mm. gunners, July 13. Octofoil insignia of 9th Infantry Division is just visible on soldier on right.

Free French troops land in Normandy.

Action was still proceeding on the St. Lô front. The 14th was the date when the U.S. 35th Inf. Div. was to make its attack to secure Hill 122, north of St. Lô. An inexperienced division, the 35th had a reputation of being well trained. However, events had shown that that reputation was meaningless since other divisions had received their first combat in Normandy with the same advance publicity and had fallen well short of expectations. This time, however, the division lived up to its pre-combat reputation. The 137th Regiment began the attack down the east bank of the Vire River, assisted by the 30th Division on the other bank. They reached the Pont-Hebert—St. Lô road west of St. Lô and were heartened by indications that their opponents had about had enough. They were fighting against the *352d Inf. Div.*, the same outfit which had given the 1st and 29th Divisions such difficulty on D-Day and immediately thereafter. It, like all of the other German divisions which had been in the fighting since the beginning, was worn down to a nub. The troops had been subjected to heavy artillery fire for three days prior to this attack and the combination of the shelling plus their depleted strength had taken much of the starch out of the *352d*.

The struggle for Hill 112 continued unabated with the Germans still in control but suffering greater and greater losses due to the incessant artillery pounding the British were directing against the hill.

At the same time, preparations for Goodwood were well underway. The British had three armoured divisions available to lead the attack—the 11th, which had made the first try for Hill 112; the 7th, equipped with the light Cromwell tanks, no match for the anticipated German defenses; and the Guards Armoured Division, newly arrived. The objective was the town of Bourgebus, which commanded two national highways, N 13, leading to Paris, and N 158, to Falaise. The tanks were expected to make a full-blooded charge. About halfway to their objective, they would outrun the range of their supporting artillery and would have to go the rest of the way supported only by their own assets. British intelligence suggested that the German defenses were only four to six kilometers deep and that there were few reserves behind them. All of this would be complemented by a major aerial bombardment which would far surpass that inflicted on Caen as part of Charnwood.

Critical to the plan was the concentration of the armoured divisions without the Germans being warned. Therefore, they were moved individually and by night to their positions.

Further, to ensure that the Germans were fixed in their positions, the new Canadian II Corps, as well as Canadian 2d Inf. Div., would attack at the same time, thereby preventing the Germans from withdrawing troops from around Caen to counter the drive of the tanks.

Free French troops pass through recently liberated town.

U.S. soldiery with abandoned German "kettenkrad" light towing vehicle.

July 15, 1944 D + 39

Since any breakout for the Americans depended on securing a position around St. Lô, the Americans adjusted their forces on the 15th, with VII Corps taking over a new sector. In addition, the 1st Inf. Div. was pulled out of the line, as was the 3d Armored, as the armored forces were brought up to strength for Cobra.

In the meantime, the drive on St. Lô continued. The Germans had added reserves to help the *352d Inf. Div.* hold off the 137th Regiment of the 35th Inf. Div., but while that regiment was being bogged down, Gerhardt sent the 134th Inf. Rgt on to Hill 122 and by sundown, it was in American hands. The 35th's actions during these two days were in very pleasant contrast to the past experience with "unblooded" units. They reacted well, did not display the loss of cohesion which seemed so typical of units not previously in combat and, obviously, performed their mission. To the division's credit, this was, in part, due to the fact that they had been in France for some time prior to going into combat and had paid close attention to the lessons being learned on the line, especially by new divisions.

At the same time, the 29th was continuing the attack along the Martinsville Ridge and the 2d Battalion of the 116th broke through to take La Madeleine, a little more than a kilometer from St. Lô. However the Germans managed to cut off the battalion from the rest of the regiment and for two days it was isolated.

Likewise, for the British the 15th was moving day as they began bringing their armored divisions into position for Goodwood.

July 16, 1944 D + 40

The American effort to secure the St. Lô-Périers road jumped off with VII Corps taking the lead. The VII Corps now had control of 30th Infantry Division, in addition to the 4th, 9th and 83d Infantry which they had had in the previous phase of the operation. To XIX Corps fell the task of trying to take St. Lô itself. At the same time, V Corps was also to push south with the result that there would be continuous pressure on the Germans all along the line, making it impossible for them to shift forces.

On the other hand, VIII Corps was in a holding mode. Even at that, the Germans were unable to undertake any adjustment of troops out of VIII Corps' sector. In fact they were busy consolidating the remnants of the divisions which had fought there into something which looked like a full division in strength. Under the designation of *91st Infantry Division* fell not only what was left of the *91st*, but also remnants of the *77th* and a kampfgruppe of which was all that remained of the *265th Inf. Div. Panzer Lehr* included a kampfgruppe from *275th Inf. Div.* No division facing the Americans was up to strength.

The isolation of 2d Battalion, 116th Infantry at La Madeleine proved, ironically, a positive factor for the Americans. The Germans, of course, attempted to eliminate this pocket. They were unable to do so. That fact alone underscored how badly the German fighting power had been reduced and, in turn, gave the Americans good reason for optimism.

July 17, 1944 D + 41

The 29th Inf. Div. broke through the German resistance around the "lost battalion" 2d Battalion, 116th Inf. Regt. At the same time, Gerhardt sent his remaining regiment, the 115th, to attack between Hill 122 and the Martinville Ridge toward St. Lô, supported by a task force under Brig. Gen. Cota, the Assistant Division Commander of the 29th Infantry Division.

On the west of St. Lô, the 330th Inf. Rgt., part of the 83d Inf. Div., had been fighting along the east bank of the Taute River and finally drew close enough to the St. Lô—Périers road so that it was decided to send the 9th Inf. Div. on a sweep of the Terrette Valley. This valley had provided a defensive position from which the Germans had harried the flanks of both the 9th and 30th Inf. Divs.

On July 17, Gfm Erwin Rommel, commander of *Heeresgruppe B*, came to the headquarters of *II SS-Panzer Corps* to meet with Bittrich, the corps commander, as well as Sepp Dietrich, commander of *I SS-Panzer Corps*, which had the direct responsibility for defense of what was left in German hands in Caen. Rommel left around 1600 to get back to his headquarters in La Roche-Guyon. En route Rommel's staff car was attacked by two fighter-bombers. Both Rommel and his driver were wounded. The car went out of control and crashed. Rommel was thrown clear but seriously injured. Although at first it was thought he might not live, he managed to begin a slow recovery. However due to events which were about to occur, Rommel never resumed command of *HG B*. Some would argue that in the few moments of that strafing run by the two fighter-bombers, the Germans lost their best chance of stopping the Allies.

July 18, 1944 D + 42

The push by Maj. Gen. Gerhardt's right flank regiment against St. Lô proved successful. Without Hill 122, the defenses in front of St. Lô could not hold off the pressure from the 29th Inf. Div. and on the 18th the Americans entered St. Lô from the north.

For the British, the 18th was the start of Operation Goodwood, to capture the remainder of Caen and secure the high ground to the south of the city, their original D-Day objective. British efforts at surprise had been unsuccessful. Vigorous German reconnaissance efforts had pretty well fixed that there would be a major attack on the 18th which would fall against the *16th Luftwaffe Field Division*, now opposing the British east of the Orne River.

At 0230, the British tanks began to move up to the lanes in the minefield and two hours later bagan to move through them. With three armoured divisions involved in the attack, they were all put under command of VIII Corps which, in effect, became an armored corps for the duration of the battle. At 0500 the air attacks went in. The effect of this bombing, was devastating. The *16th Luftwaffe Field Division*, which had been badly handled during the fighting for Caen in Charnwood, was virtually combat ineffective due to the shock effect of the bombing which lasted until 0745, at which time the artillery began its barrage. Unfortunately, some of the artillery rounds landed right in the middle of the lead elements of the 3d Royal Tank Regiment, killing several crewmen and starting the advance with considerable disorder. The tanks had hardly begun to advance when they encountered bomb craters which could not be crossed. In trying to get around them, tanks became disoriented and the whole momentum began to bog down. Worse, the reserve regiment, the 23d Hussars, found themselves a mile behind the lead regiment when they finally cleared the minefield, instead of the few hundred meters which had been planned.

The infantry, moving out on the east flank of the armored force, ran into resistance at Touffreville and fell behind schedule. Likewise, the Canadian 3d Division, which was on the west flank of the armored advance, met stiff resistance from elements of the *21st Panzer* in Colombelles.

The armored advance went well until they reached the village of Cagny where they met that nemesis of the British since D-Day, *Kampfgruppe Luck*, part of the *21st Panzer*. The kampfgruppe was augmented by the *503d Heavy Panzer Battalion*, with its Tigers and Königstigers.

The British tanks had been instructed to drive to the rear and not bother with clearing towns encountered on the way—all resistance was to be by-passed wherever possible. Accoringly, Oberst (Colonel) von Luck, the kampfgruppe commander realized he would have a chance to fire into the flanks of this armor drive and disrupt it. Moreover, the British had no infantry with their tanks. Within seconds, a company of 2d Fife and Forfar Yeomanry tanks was destroyed. The battle lasted until 1600 when some British infantry arrived and quickly captured the town. The Germans lacked infantry themselves and the damage they were able to do was only possible because the British tank forces lacked the infantry to ferret the Germans out of the town. Once the infantry arrived, success was swift.

More serious was the fact that the 3d Royal Tank Regiment, the lead battalion, found the *200th Sturmgeschütz Battalion* across its path. A sturmgeschutz was nothing more than a tur-retless tank chassis with a heavy gun mounted on it. That gave it a low profile. It was designed to give support for infantry assaulting fortified positions and therefore didn't have very heavy armor, but could do rather well against tanks because of the calibre of its gun.

With considerable effort the 3d RTR worked their way through the sturmgeschutz battalion without actually knocking it out since they were still under orders to by-pass resistance. As they got within 3000 meters of the ridgeline which was their objective, it appeared undefended, as British intelligence had suggested it would be. However, there were Germans there and they allowed the British to move to within point blank range before they opened fired. The 2d Fife & Forfar was especially badly handled. By the time the reserve regiment, the 23d Hussars, arrived, the 2d F & F had only eighteen tanks operational out of its original 52. What they had run into was *1st SS-Panzer Division*, which had been deliberately put in that position in anticipation of the British attack, to be available as a reserve. Instead it ended up being a rock against which the British wave of armor was breaking. Just before dark, the *1st SS-Panzer* launched a counterattack. While coming out of their positions caused them to suffer some tank losses, it also forced the British to break off for the day and fall back, having failed to gain their key objective.

The Canadians were rather more successful. They now had another Canadian division committed, the 2d, a veteran of the ill-fated Dieppe landings in 1942, and were under their own corps command. Their mission was to secure the factory region around Colombelles and despite resistance, worked their way into the area.

The British had put a stockpile of tanks in place for this operation and were prepared to accept heavy losses in exchange for wearing down German armor. In fact, the British lost 200 tanks on the 18th and cost the Germans very few. However, more German tanks broke down due to lack of adequate maintenance than were knocked out in combat, particularly the Tigers of *503d Heavy Tank Battalion*, which were always maintenance nightmares.

U.S. 4th Division infantryman with abandoned German
panzerfausts. Such close-quarters anti-tank weapons were
especially deadly in the bocage country.

July 19, 1944 D + 43

The failure to secure Bourgubus Ridge on the 18th led to considerable embarrassment because Montgomery had caused a message to be sent back to Britain claiming "complete success" and listing towns which had fallen, even though two were in fact still strongly defended and in German hands. For the news media in Britain, the notion that the Second Army had broken through led to a flood of commentary as if a second El Alamein had been achieved.

During the night the 3d RTR received eleven tanks, which brought them to a total of 25, about half-strength. Nonetheless, they moved off at 0430 to resume the attack on the ridge with the objective of occupying Bras and Hubert Folie. However, once they drew within range of the German guns on the ridge, they again came under heavy fire and the attack stalled. At 1500 they received word that they were to make a new push commencing at 1600, with the goal of taking Hubert Folie. The 2d Northamptonshire Yeomanry, the division reconnaissance battalion, was to give covering fire and attempt to take Bras. Artillery had been moved forward so that they would not have to make their attacks without any suppression of the German defenses. This time they not only had a good artillery barrage plus smoke to conceal their movements, but they were also supported by motorized infantry from the King's Royal Rifle Corps. By 1900 they had driven the *1st SS-Panzer* elements out of Bras. However, by the end of the day's fighting, the 29th Armoured Brigade was combat ineffective. Out of the 25 tanks in 3d RTR, only nine were left. The Fife & Forfar battalion was similarly ground down by combat.

Although 11th Armoured had the lead, the other two divisions had done little better. The 7th Armoured had not managed to get any assistance to the 11th until around 1700 on the 18th and this was only in the form of a single battalion which had managed to get through the traffic jam at the Orne. The Guards Armoured Division lost 60 tanks in its first day of fighting, about half the total lost by the 11th Armoured Division.

The Canadians were more successful, though also at a horrendous cost. The Canadian II Corps was running what amounted to a sideshow to the tank thrust, named Operation Atlantic, and it cost 1,965 casualties. The primary weight of fighting had fallen on the Canadian 2d Division, which had led with its 4th and 6th Brigades. From those brigades, in turn, the biggest losses were in the South Saskatchewan Rgt and the Essex Scottish Rgt, which lost 215 men and 244, respectively.

In the American sector, operations were still underway by the 9th Inf. Div. to clear the Germans out of the area north of the Périers—St. Lô road.

July 20, 1944 D + 44

In history, July 20, 1944 will best be remembered as the day of the abortive attempt to assassinate Hitler at his East Prussia headquarters. However, the ripples that went through the highest levels of command on the 20th were not actually felt down on the line.

With the 9th Inf. Div. having finished its clearing operations, Bradley was ready to halt in place and prepare for Operation Cobra. The front line troops were brought up to snuff as much as possible through replacements of both personnel and equipment and rested, again to the extent rest is possible for a unit on the line.

On July 20 it rained in the Normandy area and that not only ensured that Cobra would not go off on the 20th, as Bradley had originally hoped, it also served to drive the last nails in Operation Goodwood. By that time the Germans had concentrated *21st Panzer Division* plus the *1st* and *12th SS-Panzer,* and the *272d Infantry* in front of the British efforts to gain the Bourgebus Ridge.

By the 20th, the focus had shifted to the Canadian efforts and, specifically, Verrieres Ridge. It was not until almost dark that it was secured. At the same time, the 7th Armoured finally got into action, attacking the Bourgebus Ridge with some, but not much, success. They got a toehold on the ridge but could not gain complete control of it.

Although the Canadians continued to push ahead, Goodwood had essentially ended. For the Americans it presented serious concerns since their planned attack, Cobra, would also be on a narrow front and there was nothing to promise that they would not encounter the same traffic jams as the British, or that the Germans would not be able to stop them just as they had the British.

CHAPTER VIII

COBRA AND BEYOND

With the launching of Operation Cobra, the battle for Normandy effectively ended and a new, much larger battle began—that for France.

Cobra began with a major bombing attack west of St. Lô and just south of the St. Lô—Périers road. A strip approximately seven km wide was to be hit by more than 1,800 bombers. The original starting date was July 24 but more bad weather forced the bombers to turn back, moving the start to July 25.

The Americans were cagier about their operations than the British. They remained in place until almost the last minute. The Germans reported a considerable concentration of American troops the previous day, but around 0700, they began to fall back. Before the Germans could take advantage of it by moving forward, as they had against the British, the bombers were upon them. The first attacks began at 0938 with the fighter-bombers. Bradley had asked that the attacks be run from east to west, parallel with the front, to avoid any short bombs hitting the American troops but the bombers made their run from north to south and there were some very serious losses among the front line units. Moreover, once the bombing ended and the units of VII Corps began to move out, they found that *Panzer Lehr*, in their path, had not been destroyed but only battered around some. What did make a difference was that though the Germans resisted strongly, their defensive positions were not prepared in depth nor linked laterally the way they had been in front of British Second Army during Goodwood. As a result, the Americans could get around the defenses and by-pass them as necessary.

A key element were those tanks which came to be known as Rhinos—tanks with the Cullin Hedgerow device welded on the front. This allowed the American tanks to move across country while the Germans, lacking them, were forced to keep their tanks road bound. This meant the ideal situation for tanks—fairly level ground and nothing but infantry in the way. It would take a Rhino tank about two and a half minutes to break through a hedgerow, as opposed to hours for normally equipped tanks.

By the end of the 25th, there were clear indications that the American infantry had gotten through the defenses of most of *Panzer Lehr* and the armored divisions were now committed. They ran as fast and as far as they could. It is an axiom of armored warfare that once a penetration is made, the tanks should run to the rear, disrupt rearward communications and supplies, and keep on running. The infantry will shore up the shoulders and roll back the flanks of the units through which the tanks have passed. This leaves the enemy two choices. If he has enough strength to counterattack, it is possible to cut off the tank penetration but if he doesn't, then he faces a larger and deeper hole in his lines the longer he waits—he must fall back and do so rapidly. By 0300 on the 26th, Combat Command A of 2d Arm. Div. had reached a road junction north of Le Mesnil-Herman, the first objective of Cobra. By 1200 of the 27th, even the infantry was now fighting clear of the German defenses and they were able to advance rapidly forward. In fact, their biggest problem was that the German rear areas were now in total chaos as stragglers and troops trying to get back from the front to form up a new line were all over, without any organized pattern to where they might next appear. By the 29th, Combat Command B of 4th Armored Division was at Coutances.

Cobra was what the Allies had wanted for over a month. It literally tore open the German defenses and by the time anything like a front had been established, the Germans had lost what possible chance they may have had of containing the Allies in Normandy. Worse was in store for the Germans. On August 1, the U.S. Third Army became operational under Lt. Gen. George S. Patton, Jr.—just the man to chase the German left flank, ripped open by Cobra, over much of France.

U.S. soldiers cut up German beach obstacles to make hedgerow plow blades.

U.S. 155s pound St. Lô, July 24th.

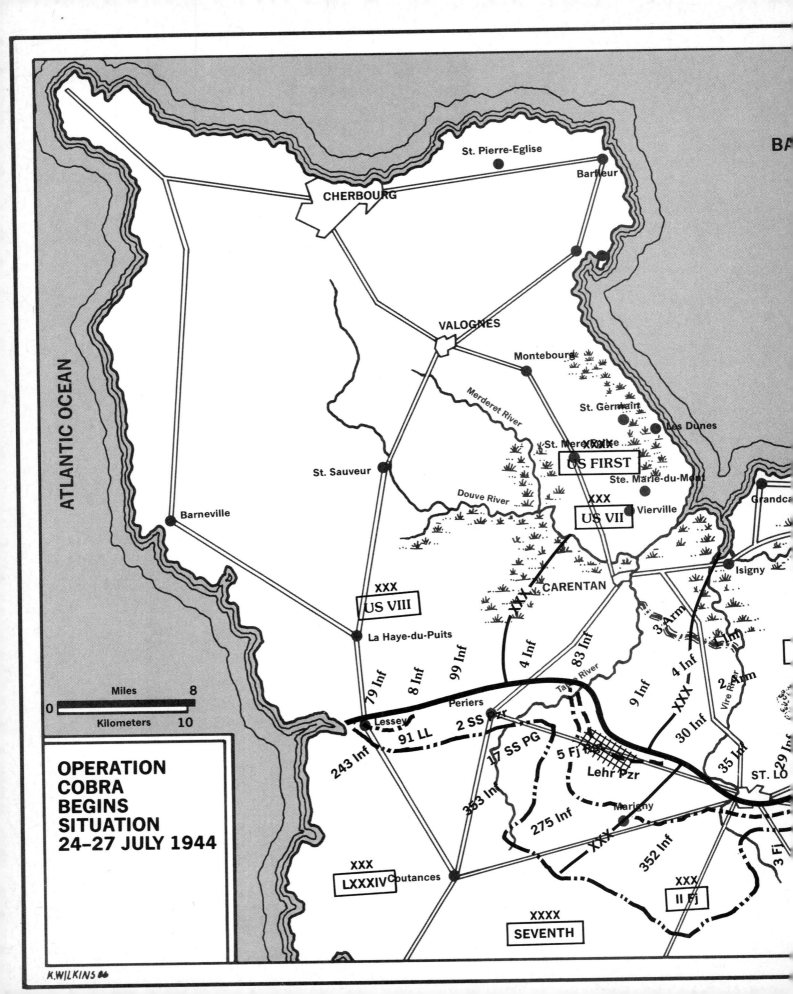

ATLANTIC OCEAN

BA

St. Pierre-Eglise

Barfleur

CHERBOURG

VALOGNES

Montebourg

Merderet River

St. Germain

Les Dunes

St. Mere-Eglise

XXX
US FIRST

St. Sauveur

Ste. Marie-du-Mont

XXX
US VII

Vierville

Grandca

Douve River

Isigny

Barneville

CARENTAN

XXX
US VIII

3. Arm

1m

La Haye-du-Puits

4 Inf

83 Inf

4 Inf

2 Arm

Tau River

Vire River

79 Inf

8 Inf

99 Inf

9 Inf

XXX

Miles   8
0
Kilometers   10

Periers

Pzr

30 Inf

35 Inf

ST. LO

Lessey

91 LL

2 SS

17 SS PG

5 Fj

Lehr Pzr

243 Inf

**OPERATION
COBRA
BEGINS
SITUATION
24–27 JULY 1944**

353 Inf

275 Inf

Marigny

352 Inf

3 Fj

XXX
LXXXIV C Coutances

XXX
II Fj

XXXX
SEVENTH

K.WILKINS 86

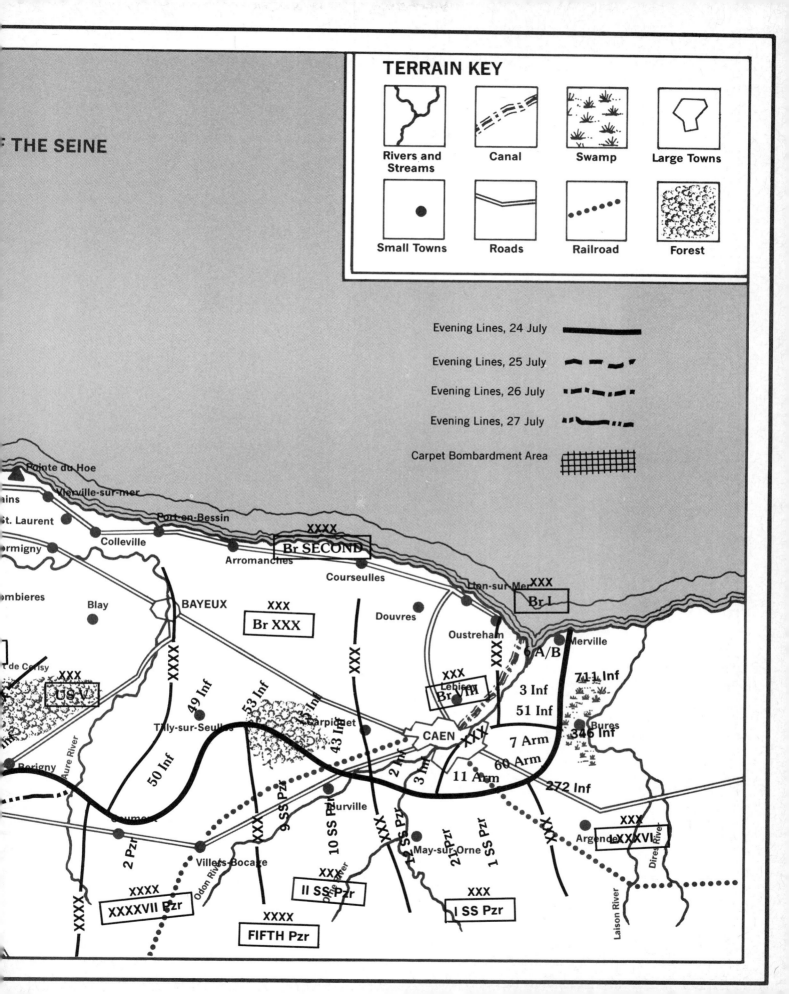

TERRAIN KEY

Rivers and Streams	Canal	Swamp	Large Towns
Small Towns	Roads	Railroad	Forest

Evening Lines, 24 July ▬▬▬▬

Evening Lines, 25 July ▬ ▬ ▬

Evening Lines, 26 July ▬·▬·▬

Evening Lines, 27 July ▬ ▬ ▬

Carpet Bombardment Area ▦

F THE SEINE

Pointe du Hoe

Vierville-sur-mer

ains

St. Laurent

Port-en-Bessin

Colleville

Courseulles

XXXX
Br SECOND

ormigny

Arromanches

Lion-sur-Mer **XXX**
Br I

ombieres

Blay

BAYEUX

XXX
Br XXX

Douvres

Oustreham

Merville

711 Inf

t de Corsy

XXX
US V

49 Inf

Tilly-sur-Seulles

53 Inf

Carpiquet

43 Inf

CAEN

XXX
Br VIII

Lebisen

3 Inf

51 Inf

Bures

346 Inf

7 Arm

Perigny

Aure River

50 Inf

2 Pzr

Villers-Bocage

Odon River

9 SS Pzr

10 SS Pzr

Hurville

12 SS Pzr

60 Arm

11 Arm

272 Inf

2 Inf

3 Inf

May-sur-Orne

1 SS Pzr

21 Pzr

Argentan

XXX
XXXVI

Dives River

XXXX
XXXXVII Pzr

XXX
II SS Pzr

XXXX
FIFTH Pzr

XXX
I SS Pzr

Laison River

9th Division bazooka team during the breakout, August 15th.

Summary

The events of June 6, 1944, are among the great events of history. In a very real sense, for the western Allies, this was the formal beginning of the end for Nazi Germany. Only the Ardennes Offensive of December, 1944, ranks anywhere near D-Day in popular imagination. The month and half which followed, however, was anything but a spectacular success for the Allies. In fact, a day-by-day account of the operations in Normandy appears, at times, to be an unrelenting record of lost chances and miscues. At the outset it should be noted that at the time it was one of a very few successful amphibious operations ever conducted in the history of warfare. It was, without a doubt, the largest amphibious force ever landed anywhere. Throughout all of this period supply was strictly over the beaches, and through Mulberry B, because the Allies lacked a major port. Moreover, whatever the benefits of landing in Normandy from the vantage of gaining surprise, the terrain, especially the bocage, favored the defenders—whichever side was on the defense at any time. Yet, despite all of those disadvantages, the Allies managed to overcome the defenders.

There were shortcomings. Unquestionably the British were too tentative. There was a serious concern that the British were coming to the end of their manpower and simply could not afford the losses which the Americans could and hence they were reluctant to risk taking too many casualties. Moreover, no operation was begun except in anticipation that it would succeed. However, it is clear that in almost every case, the British were always a little too light to crack the German defenses. As a result, it is not invalid to argue that the British might have done much better had they accepted heavy casualties at first and pressed forward all along their front, early on, before the Germans had shored up their defenses. In the end, they still took heavy losses in personnel and had nothing to show for it. There were many instances when it was clear they were going toe-to-toe with a German unit and virtually wearing it out when they could have broken loose another British division to

4th Infantry Division mortar in action, July 26th. The ever-present bocage hedgerows, such as the one in the background, made high-angle weapons like mortars even more valuable.

take advantage of so many units being tied down. The Americans uniformly made broader front attacks, once they got established.

From a British point of view, there were several mistakes which simply should and could have been avoided. The traffic jam at Cheux which destroyed Epsom was unpredictable but to repeat the same problem in Goodwood made no sense at all. It is apparent that no one took the time to compute a probable traffic flow—the movement times were essentially arbitrary, classroom type determinations. The two largest operations the British conducted in the period, Epsom and Goodwood, ended up with considerable amounts of combat strength tied up behind the lead element. As a result, in the earliest fighting, when the advantage of surprise is with the attacker, the British were allowing the defender time to react rather than being able to pour all of their strength forward at once. That was purely a planning fault. Simplicity is a maxim of military operations and history has shown that the more complex a plan is, the surer it is that something will go amiss.

It is hard to say whether the British were simply more careless than the Americans or the Germans more aggressive in their reconnaissance and more accurate in their intelligence assessments, but it appears that the British fatally telegraphed their punches. In Epsom the Germans were indeed reading British radio traffic and knew a great deal about what was going on. For Goodwood, Dietrich later claimed that he simply did a trick he learned in Russia—put his ear to the ground. Whatever, the fact is that the British were plagued by having to attack a defender who was usually on the alert.

For the Americans, the first obvious point is that no one took the bocage seriously enough because they were woefully unready to deal with it. The whole history of the American operations in the bocage, with the brief period of the drive to the west coast and on to Cherbourg, was fighting the hedgerows. In some respects, they were a bigger enemy than the Germans.

A second American weakness was a short fuse with commanders who did not immediately succeed. It appeared that the old maxim about initial impressions counted. If a commander jumped off with good results in the first few days of fighting, any problems he had after that were attributed to factors beyond his control. If he jumped off poorly, he was fired. This was so even when a neighboring division was doing no better but had the earlier good reputation. The 90th Infantry Division was deemed ill-

led in the efforts to break out of the Utah lodgement but right next to it was the 82d Airborne, which was doing no better, but which had already made its reputation.

If any army comes off well in the fighting in Normandy, it must be the Germany Army. The commanders were all experienced and even though some units were not expected to fight very well, there were few cases of people giving up and running. Every inch gained by the Allies was, by and large, hard earned. Moreover, if anything won the fighting in Normandy for the Allies, it was not superior skills but simply supe-

U.S. 28th Infantry Division passes under the arch of Triumph August 29, 1944.

rior numbers. By the time Cobra was launched, the real strength had been bled out of the German divisions on the western side. There was really no German reserve, in the true sense of a force large enough to influence the fighting. At best the reserve was a fire brigade to be thrown in where the front line units could not longer hold. The ability of 150 members of *12th SS-Panzer* division to hold off a brigade of Canadians at Carpiquet is a good example of how well the German army fought. Again, in the end, pure numbers told. Once the crust of the German defense was broken, as finally happened in

Cobra, the outcome was inevitable. Indeed, that could well sum up the rest of the fighting against Germany. Right up to the end, statistics showed that man for man, the Germans inflicted more casualties on the Allies than they received. The Americans lost 40,000 men from July 1 to July 20. That is the equivalent of about three infantry divisions. They could afford to replace them and the Germans could not. There were simply so many more Allied units that German ability was overwhelmed.

D-Day Deception and Beyond

The Allies knew that the Germans would try to stop any invasion close to the beaches. This would be the time when the whole operation was the most vulnerable. If they got a deep enough lodgement and had enough troops ashore, the Allies would be back on the continent to stay. It would be the first few days and weeks which would tell the story.

Accordingly, it was imperative to try to divert as many troops from the landing area as possible and also to pin down any potential reinforcements. Operation "Fortitude" was the first step, begun well before the landings. The objective there was to make the Germans think that there was a "First U.S. Army Group" stationed in eastern England, under command of Lt. Gen. George S. Patton, Jr., with the mission of making the main Allied landings at the Pas de Calais. However, deceiving the Germans as to the initial point of landing was seen as the easy part. The difficult phase would be to confuse them as to what was going ashore in Normandy. More immediate to their needs, they also had to find a way to keep the Germans confused about the scope of the landings in Normandy. Was it the main invasion or only a feint?

"Titanic" was the codename given one of the cover plans. It was not only deceptively obvious, but guaranteed to embarrass the Germans. The human element involved dropping a few British Commandos, equipped with record players and amplifiers. When they landed, they would turn on the record players and play the sounds of soldiers parachuting in, complete with appropri-

ate profanity. They would also set off smoke grenades to create the effect of battle smoke. The key element, however, were half-size dummies which would be dropped by the hundreds, complete with their own parachutes, so that they could be seen dropping just as if they were real paratroopers. They would be dropped outside of the basic landing areas in hopes of tricking the Germans into diverting troops to deal with these "landings." The dummies also added to the sounds of combat by ejecting pintail bombs which would shoot up parachute flares and Very lights. Finally, the same planes which dropped the dummies would drop machinegun and rifle fire simulators to make a very real combat sound for anyone around to hear. One such drop occured west of St. Lô, others as Yvetot, Harfleur,, near Le Havre, between Lisieux and Evreaux, near Lessay, Villedicu-les-Poeles and St. Hilaire-du-Harcourt, as well as around the Forêt d'Ecouves and the Forêt de Cerisy.

Titanic had an immediate effect. Von Rundstedt ordered a major portion of the *12th SS-Panzer Division* to go to Lisieux and deal with the parachutists; most of the *352d*'s reserve regiment was also sent to deal with another such "drop."

The following day, June 7, a report came in of yet another airborne drop in the Coutances-Lessay area, west of St. Lô. Fearing it was a prelude to a second landing, on the west side of the peninsula, Rommel ordered reserves being brought up from the west to detour through that area to deal with the paratroopers. In fact, it was just another

phase of Titanic, still working its magic.

To add to the confusion, starting at 0930, the British Broadcasting Company began to transmit messages from the leaders of the various governments-in-exile announcing that a landing had been made. However, as part of the deception, all of these speeches deliberately referred to this as an initial landing and made reference to it being part of a grand strategic plan. Each speech told the local resistance to keep calm and take no action so that when the "critical moment" came, they would be available. Even the British Parliament was kept in the dark as Churchill, adressing them, announced that this was the first of a series of landings designed to liberate Europe and that "in this case, the liberating assault fell on the coast of France." The implication that, in the "next case" it would fall on some other country's coast was clear.

What Luftwaffe activity there was in northern France was kept busy by deceptive imitation, the procedure whereby a German-speaking British transmitter would talk to the German aircraft on their control frequencies and misdirect them, often to the point of explicitly countermanding orders just given by the genuine controllers and claiming that the genuine controllers were actually British engaging in deception measures.

The over-all result could not have been better. The German high command was paralyzed and took no action until it was too late, convinced that Normandy was only the first, and probably the lightest, of several blows which would fall.